FIGHTING IMPUNIT_

A guide on how civil society can use Magnitsky Acts to sanction human rights violators

Published in the United States by Safeguard Defenders

First edition.

Keywords: Magnitsky Act, Human Rights, Criminal Justice, International law, Impunity

Also available as paperback and Kindle e-book on Amazon worldwide:

ISBN: 978-0-9993706-9-8

This guide is available, for free, in localized versions, and can be found on the website below. Chinese (simplified) edition will be released shortly after the English edition, with other localized versions being released step by step.

https://SafeguardDefenders.com

PART I - The Basics

PART II - The Process

PART III - The Submission

PART IV - Investigative Techniques

PART V - Post-Submission/Advocacy

Additional Information

Appendices

Readers' guide

The guide seeks to show, in the easiest yet still detailed enough way, how to effectively use the growing list of Magnitsky acts in different countries (jurisdictions). So far, the United States, the United Kingdom and Canada are the three jurisdictions most likely to be useful to defend human rights in China, but the three Baltic States and Gibraltar has also implemented Magnitsky laws. Importantly, other key jurisdictions, such as Australia and the EU are both close to creating Magnitsky laws.

Sergei Magnitsky was a Russian lawyer who, after working to expose corruption, was tortured to death in a Russian detention center. The laws are often called Magnitsky acts in his honor, but have different names in different countries.

The Magnitsky acts are groundbreaking, and potentially very powerful, because individuals can be targeted. If you can pinpoint an individual as having committed, or ordered (command responsibility) any gross human rights violation or corruption, you can ask these jurisdictions above to sanction that individual, from assets freezing to travel bans. It is especially useful in countries like Russia and China (target countries), where the spoils of corruption are often moved abroad, and can be targeted.

This guide is divided into five sections, and shows the work needed to file someone for sanctioning (submission), both before (Part 1 – the Basics), how the process works (Part 2 – the Process), how to write and structure the submission (Part 3 – the Submission), and what you can do after the submission (Part 5 – Post-Submission/Advocacy). It also includes a China-specific research guide (Part 4 – Investigative Techniques) for how to identify perpetrators.

Due to Magnitsky acts being new there are a lot of unknowns. Add to this that political considerations are not only important, but crucial, to have any jurisdiction take action against a powerful country like China – this guide has been made possible only due to significant input from diplomats, government workers, people involved in the actual drafting of the laws, as well as international organizations that either works with the laws. To ensure strong input, full anonymity has been offered, to have as candid and frank discussions as possible. It is because of this we can now present this full-fledged guide.

As some countries, like the UK, will not start using sanctioning until after Brexit, while others are still developing practical routines, yet others are about to create Magnitsky acts, this document will be further updated, to take new developments into account.

PART I - THE BASICS

1.1 What is a Magnitsky Act?

The Magnitsky Act is a powerful tool found in a growing number of jurisdictions across the globe (currently: the U.S., Canada, UK, Gibraltar, Estonia, Latvia and Lithuania), which allows governments to sanction individuals and companies/groups outside their legal jurisdiction for serious human rights violations and corruption. Depending on the jurisdiction, these sanctions can include asset freezes and/or travel bans.

For example, the U.S. could sanction a Chinese official living in China for carrying out serious human rights abuses against Chinese citizens (such as torture, extrajudicial killing, rape, enforced disappearance) by having his or her financial assets seized in the U.S. and banned from entering the country. This also applies to those responsible for having ordered any such action (those with command responsibility).

Research undertaken by civil society to document abuses often serves as an important source of evidence that governments use against perpetrators in issuing sanctions. Some jurisdictions even allow civil society to directly file submissions for sanctions.

The process of imposing a Magnitsky sanction from a civil society filing generally follows the path shown in the figure below:

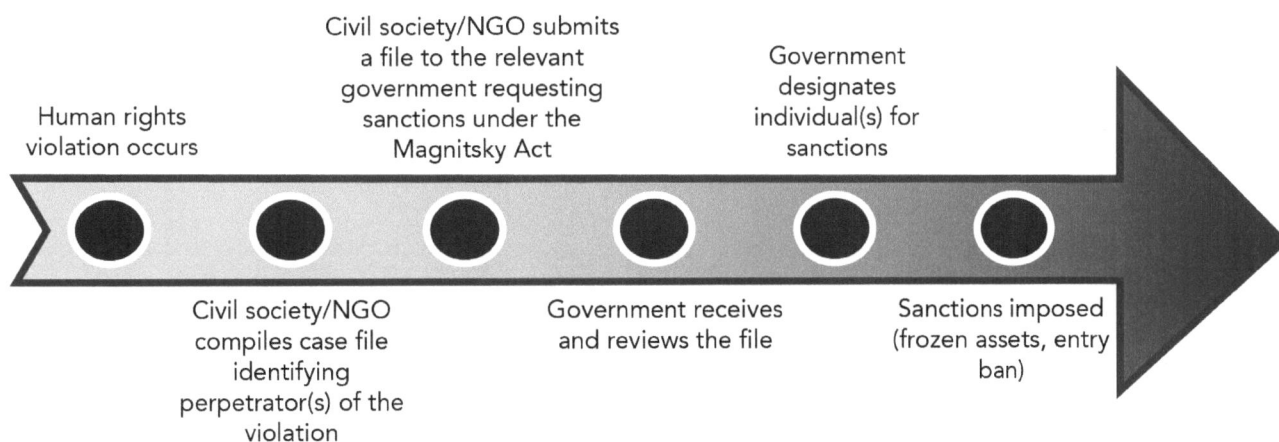

Human rights violation occurs

Civil society/NGO compiles case file identifying perpetrator(s) of the violation

Civil society/NGO submits a file to the relevant government requesting sanctions under the Magnitsky Act

Government receives and reviews the file

Government designates individual(s) for sanctions

Sanctions imposed (frozen assets, entry ban)

These acts go by different official names but are referred to commonly here as "Magnitsky Acts" given their similarity in purpose and origin. These Acts take their name from the Russian lawyer Sergei Magnitsky who was murdered by Russian officials after uncovering corrupt practices.

Other jurisdictions are considering similar legislation, such as the Netherlands and Australia, as well as the European Union.

1.2 What impacts can a Magnitsky Act have?

Magnitsky Acts directly punish perpetrators of human rights violations (those who carried out the violation, those who ordered the violation, or those who provided assistance to the perpetrators) when that country's legal system fails to hold them accountable. Being placed on a country's list of Magnitsky designations can have several direct impacts.

1. Financial loss. Several jurisdictions (the U.S., UK, Canada and Gibraltar) permit the freezing of the perpetrator's assets that are located within its financial system. Since countries like the U.S., UK and Canada are important financial centers, this could result in significant losses to the perpetrator sanctioned. In particular, any designation made by the U.S. may also affect the perpetrator's finances in other countries since many banks will not want to risk doing business with someone sanctioned by the U.S.

2. Travel ban. Perpetrators denied entry will have any existing visa revoked and will be barred from entering the country until the designation is removed.

3. Shame. The designation may have a powerful public shaming effect on the perpetrator and damage their reputation. In addition, they could lose financial or business opportunities if international businesses and banks shun the perpetrator or entity to avoid being associated with human rights violators. Thus, there are financial implications even if the jurisdiction does not impose an asset freeze.

Most importantly, Magnitsky Acts could help push systemic change in countries and regions where human rights abuses are common. Indeed, the primary purpose of these acts is not to punish violators, but rather to impose sanctions in order to deter similar behavior in the future. Thus, even though many petitions will be unsuccessful, there are greater benefits to the wider human rights community that can be gained through these mechanisms.

This can include directly ordering others to commit the violation; not having acted to stop the violation despite evidence they knew it was occurring; not having held the perpetrators responsible after learning about the violation; and not having provided proper medical treatment to the victim after the violation took place.

An important additional element of these sanctions is that they allow targeted action to be taken against those who are directly responsible for the human rights violations rather than countrywide sanctions that impact all citizens regardless of whether or not they played a role in the violation.

Who was Sergei Magnitsky?

Magnitsky Acts derive their name from Sergei Magnitsky, a Russian lawyer who was killed in 2009 while being detained by Russian security forces for exposing fraud committed by government officials.

Magnitsky was working as a tax lawyer for the Moscow office of legal and audit firm Firestone Duncan when he discovered that senior officials at the Interior Ministry had stolen 5.4 billion rubles (approximately U.S.$230 million) from one of his clients – the investment firm Hermitage Capital Management – as well as the Russian Treasury. Risking his own safety, Magnitsky reported the fraud. But instead of investigating, the police arrested him. During the 358 days of his detention, Magnitsky was subjected to physical and mental abuse and denied access to medical treatment. He died in detention on 16 November 2009.

His case sparked international outrage and Hermitage Capital Management's founder, Bill Browder, began lobbying foreign governments to impose sanctions against those responsible for his detention and death. Those efforts gave rise to the series of Magnitsky Acts that have been passed in the U.S., Canada, Estonia, Latvia, Lithuania, Gibraltar and the UK so far.

1.3 Who Imposes Magnitsky sanctions?

JURISDICTION	NAME OF LEGISLATION	ACCEPTED VIOLATIONS	EXAMPLES
USA	Global Magnitsky Human Rights Accountability Act Executive Order 13818: Blocking the Property of Persons Involved in Serious Human Rights Abuse or Corruption	(i) "Serious human rights abuses" (ii) Corruption	Extrajudicial killing; rape; torture; forced disappearance
UK	Criminal Finances Act 2017 Sanctions and Anti-Money Laundering Act 2018	Gross human rights abuses	Extrajudicial killing, torture, rape
CANADA	Justice for Victims of Corrupt Foreign Officials Act Justice for Victims of Corrupt Foreign Officials Regulations Special Economic Measures Act	(i) Gross violations of internationally recognized human rights (ii) Acts of "significant" corruption	Extrajudicial killing, torture, rape
ESTONIA	Act on Amendments to the Obligation to Leave and Prohibition on Entry Act	(i) Violation of human rights, resulting in death or serious injury (ii) Causing an individual to be wrongly convicted based on political motives	Extrajudicial killing, torture, rape
LATVIA	Proposal to introduce sanctions against the officials connected to the Sergei Magnitsky case	Not clear	Not clear
LITHUANIA	Amendment to the Law on the Legal Status of Aliens	Violations of human rights or freedoms in a foreign country, corruption offences, money laundering	Not clear
GIBRALTAR	The Proceeds of Crime (Amendment) Act 2018	'unlawful conduct'	Torture or degrading treatment of a person that has been defending human rights, or has sought to expose gross human rights abuse by a public official.

WHO CAN BE SANCTIONED	SANCTIONS	WHERE TO SUBMIT
Any foreign national or groups	Asset freezes Entry ban	State Department: globalmagnitsky@state.gov Treasury Department: glomag@treasury.gov
Public officials; those acting in official capacity	Asset freezes Entry ban	No procedure set up yet, pending finalization of Brexit, but will lie with the Foreign and Commonwealth office, and the Treasury office.
Any foreign national	Asset freezes Entry ban	Global Affairs Canada: sanctions@international.gc.ca
Any foreign national	Entry ban	Ministry of Foreign Affairs vminfo@vm.ee
Not clear	Entry ban	Ministry of Foreign Affairs mfa.cha@mfa.gov.lv
Any foreign national	Entry ban	Ministry of Foreign Affairs urm@urm.lt
Public officials; those acting in official capacities	Asset freezes	Royal Gibraltar Police (RGP)): info@royalgib.police.gi

1.4 Step by Step:
Making a Magnitsky submission

Example: fictionalized torture case in China

Guo Bo, an activist researching the violation of environmental regulations by local enterprises in Xifang County was seriously tortured over several days at the local detention center by the Public Security Bureau (police). Activists decide to hold the local police accountable for this gross violation of human rights by filing a request that the perpetrators be punished through Magnitsky sanctions in the U.S.

Result:

Even though they did not receive any feedback from the U.S. government on their submission, nine months after they filed it, one of the senior PSB officers, Deng was placed on the list of U.S. Magnitsky Sanctions.

F-I-N-I-S-H

Step 7: Start advocacy work

The activists begin contacting key members of the U.S. Congress who support human rights in China to lobby for Magnitsky sanctions on the four perpetrators.

Step 6: File the submission

Two ways, to either submit the file containing all evidence, translations and arguments collected in Step Five to the State Department and Treasury Department's Magnitsky Act emails, or to contact the U.S. Congress' Congressional Executive Commission on China (CECC) and ask for their help to submit it instead.

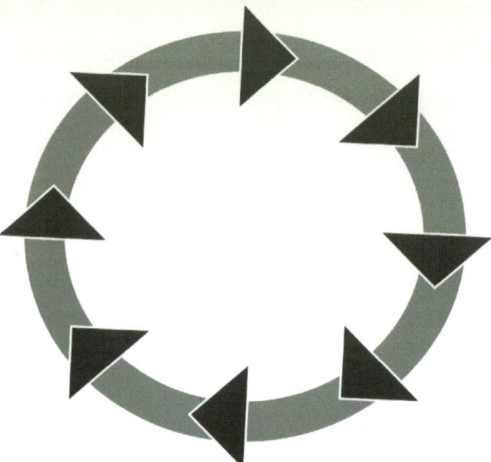

Step 5: Make clear arguments for sanctions

The activists then lay out their arguments for why imposing Magnitsky sanctions on Deng, Luo, Liu and Han could reduce the incidence of torture by Xifang PSB and more broadly across China. They argue the sanctions will serve U.S. national interests, citing Washington's China and East Asia policy and counter arguments that they could harm other U.S. objectives in the region.

Step 4: Translate all material into English

They translated all Chinese-language sources into English and added information on the translation.

Step 1: Evaluate whether the acts are covered by U.S. Magnitsky sanctions

Since "serious human rights abuses" including torture are specified under the Act, they conclude the case satisfies requirements for filing a submission for Magnitsky sanctions.

Step 2: Determine all those responsible for the torture

Using evidence given by Guo and other witnesses, they identify two police officers – Han Dan and Liu Shan – as those responsible for carrying out the acts of torture on Guo on at least three separate occasions at Xifang Detention Center.

Using the county's official PSB website, they determine that Han and Liu's superior officers at Xifang Detention Center are Deng Feng and Luo Huo. Because of the chain of command, these two individuals would have been aware of the torture, did not stop it, and very likely ordered it to be carried out.

Step 3: Collect the evidence

First, they research detailed information to accurately identify the four perpetrators. This includes their full names, dates and places of birth; ID numbers; and job titles at Xifang Detention Center.

Second, they collect as much evidence as possible to prove that Guo had been tortured. This includes testimony given by Guo to her lawyer; reports from human rights organizations (including noting the methods they used to make the torture claims); and reports from news organizations on the torture. They take care to provide both the URLs for all online material as well as screenshots for the web pages in case the Chinese government takes them offline.

Third, they collect additional evidence to prove that Deng and Luo were also responsible–this is called Command Responsibility. This includes the URL and screenshot from the official Xifang PSB website. They also describe in detail their responsibilities within the Xifang PSB and at Xifang Detention Center to prove they are indirectly responsible for the torture.

Finally, they collect supporting evidence of other examples or human rights abuses that took place at Xifang Detention Center while Deng and Luo were in charge. This would help show a pattern of behavior and that Guo's torture is not an isolated incident.

PART II - THE PROCESS

2.1 Is Magnitsky suitable for my case?

The first step should always be to figure out whether Magnitsky is right for your case.

Does the human rights violation (or act of corruption) qualify under existing legislation? As a general rule, the following qualify in any of the existing jurisdictions: extrajudicial killing, torture or rape carried out by a government official, an individual acting in an official capacity, or at the request of a government official. In some jurisdictions, additionally, the victim must have been seeking to promote or defend human rights or expose corruption by government officials. In the U.S. enforced disappearances also qualify for Magnitsky sanctions.

The next step is determine whether you can precisely identify all perpetrators. That includes those directly responsible and those with command responsibility.

It is crucial that all perpetrators are clearly identified with their full name, date of birth, place of birth and ID number.

Evidence linking the perpetrators to the violation should be objective, credible and verifiable. It should include primary sources and credible secondary sources. The Magnitsky jurisdiction should easily be able to corroborate and verify your evidence, or else it cannot act. Evidence must be clear, strong and verifiable.

For the U.S., the violation(s) should have occurred within the past five years.

In addition, your case will be stronger

if you can also prove the violation is part of a wider pattern of behavior (by the perpetrator(s), the entity they work for, or within the country as a whole).

Checklist for deciding whether your case is suitable for a Magnitsky filing

- The human rights abuse qualifies under the jurisdiction's Magnitsky Act.

- The perpetrator is not being punished or tried for the violations by either the target country or the Magnitsky jurisdiction.

- The violation(s) occurred within the past five years.

- The violation(s) are ongoing and/ or part of a pattern of behavior (ideal, but not necessary).

- The perpetrator(s) can be accurately identified.

- The perpetrator(s) is either directly responsible or has command responsibility. (Note. Command responsibility cannot extend to country leaders.)

- All evidence is credible and verifiable and includes primary sources.

If there are other sanctioning mechanisms exist (such as U.S. sanctions on Iran) it is possible the Magnitsky jurisdiction choose to make use of that mechanism instead.

[5] *Certain high profile and extreme cases may be exempted from this general rule. An example of this would be the killing of Saudi journalist Jamal Khashoggi in 2018 in Turkey.*

2.2 Where should you file?

The next step is to decide on the jurisdiction(s) that would work best for your submission. As of September 2019, there are seven jurisdictions that have Magnitsky Acts, with Australia and the EU, as well as some individual European countries, considering adopting it as well.

In selecting where to file, there are several issues to consider:

- How open is the jurisdiction to receiving submissions from civil society?

- If sanctions are imposed, which jurisdiction will have the biggest impact?

- How likely is it the jurisdiction will approve the submission given current political realities and its relationship with the target country?

A submission to the U.S. will likely have the greatest impact because:

- The U.S.' financial system is the world's biggest so sanctions would not only involve U.S. banks but many banks outside the U.S. would also elect to comply to avoid the possibility they themselves will be targeted by U.S. sanctions.

- The U.S. is more active in imposing sanctions, making it the jurisdiction most likely to take action to date.

- The U.S. has the most resources devoted to investigating cases under its Magnitsky Act.

Canada is also a good choice because it has issued Magnitsky sanctions before, including asset freezes and visa bans,

and the submission for civil society is more streamlined. Canada is also a common place for Chinese to both live, have vacation homes, or to invest. However, Canada tends to follow its allies (usually the U.S.) and might not issue sanctions against officials that haven't already been targeted. Another issue is that Canada has fewer resources so the review process may take much longer.

The UK has not yet issued any sanctions under its Magnitsky Act and it may be reluctant to use the instrument until its exit from the European Union (scheduled for 31 October 2019) is complete. At time of writing, they have not issued any procedure for how to manage submissions under the Magnitsky Act.

The Baltic Countries (Estonia, Latvia and Lithuania) may not be keen to sanction Chinese perpetrators and because of their small size the impact of visa bans may have limited impact. However, it may be worth pursuing because of the public shame factor of officially being listed as a human rights violator for the perpetrator. All three countries however do no make any information available on how civil society can or should interact with those countries, and its officials have been very slow and unresponsive to assist in clarifying that. Hence, do not focus on the Baltic States at time of writing.

To maximize your chance of success, a good approach is to submit applications to several jurisdictions simultaneously. Most of the information needed for submissions across jurisdictions are similar, requiring only minor adjustments. In general, we recommend focusing on the U.S. and Canada, and once Brexit is complete, also the UK.

Even when submissions fail – and they most often do – there are great benefits from making the filing, as it shames the named perpetrator and also puts pressure on them that future violations may be monitored and submitted for sanctions again. Others in a similar situation may likewise take notice and become under greater pressure to not undertake human rights violations.

Politics and National Interest

Ideally, Magnitsky Acts would result in sanctions against all submissions on human rights violators. In reality, governments enacted them to promote their own national interests and they are unlikely to impose sanctions unless they believe it will further these. Fortunately, in many cases, upholding human rights abroad is often seen beneficial to national interests. That is why it is crucial to argue strongly in your submission that Magnitsky sanctions are in the best interests of the jurisdiction (this is especially important for the U.S.).

These sanctions are elective, which means the jurisdiction is not obliged to act even when it confirms the violation did occur. Failure to act is usually because of political reasons. For example, the U.S. may avoid taking action against China because it is currently negotiating a trade deal with Beijing or it needs Beijing's help to pressure North Korea or backing for a UN Security Council Resolution against Iran. Instead, the U.S. may use diplomatic channels rather than sanctions in this case.

The best time to submit your Magnitsky filing may be when relations between the U.S. and the target country is at its most strained.

In your application, you should emphasize the role these sanctions would play in stopping future violations of human rights and promoting a change of behavior rather than simply arguing for punishing the perpetrators. You should provide evidence the violation is part of a wider pattern of abuse. You must argue sanctions would further the national interests of the jurisdiction and not undermine its other goals.

You will need a nuanced understanding of the jurisdiction's national security objectives and it may be helpful to team up with others to help articulate this clearly in your submission.

2.3 Identify partners before submitting

While it is possible for individuals or organizations to file, it may strengthen your application if you work with partners.

Local partners

Local partners can share ideas on how to approach the submission; they may also have special expertise or knowledge that you do not have. Investigators in the Magnitsky jurisdiction have limited resources, so a single submission from several actors can save them time and makes the filing more credible.

Foreign partners

Reach out to a foreign partner who is familiar with the Magnitsky jurisdiction. They can help navigate its institutional framework and they can advise on the politics involved and where its national interests lie. It could also assist in translating, editing and writing the submission. Governments tends to have their own language, and being able to communicate in that language can help with the submission.

In addition, foreign partners can help with post-submission advocacy. This involves lobbying politicians and requires a physical presence in the country to set up face-to-face meetings.

Human Rights First is a U.S.-based organization that can assist with submissions and advocacy. They have a working relationship with the U.S. State Department and are familiar with their staff and structure of submissions. They have a presence in Washington DC and are able to set up face-to-face meetings with State and Treasury officials as well as with Congressional members for

advocacy purposes. They can be reached at globalmagnitsky@protonmail.com.

ProtonMail is a webmail that offers strong encryption between different ProtonMail users, including self-destruct messages. It now also have a Chinese language interface. For safety, consider using a free ProtonMail account (https://protonmail.com).

2.4. Timeline

Submissions take time. You need the resources to carefully and accurately compile all the evidence and information on perpetrators before writing the submission. How long this takes depends on your resources and how difficult or easy it is to gather the evidence.

Once a submission is made, the time it takes for it to be reviewed will vary widely. In general, you should expect at least six to nine months before any action is taken. The length of time depends on how complete your submission is, the investigation required to verify the evidence, whether political considerations include diplomatic efforts to be pursued first and whether it is a priority for the government.

Note you will not be informed if your submission is unsuccessful.

The U.S. has imposed Magnitsky sanctions in as little as six weeks after the initial submission, but this is very rare. In general, the process goes through a lengthy vetting cycle on an annual basis. They review all names submitted by civil society, Congress, and internally by other government departments. Generally, this takes place in the first few months of the year so the best time to make a submission is December if you want the quickest possible designation. Anything submitted in summer will likely not be reviewed until December when the State Department has finished putting together its annual report.

2.5 Confidentiality

Governments make every effort to ensure the information provided by the party filing the submission is kept confidential. Unfortunately, since submissions usually involve email communications it is possible that this could be compromised.

Use encrypted email in all communications and always practice safe digital security.

Make it obvious that your submission contains sensitive information. Human Rights First recommends all submission emails and documents to the U.S. include a header that reads:

> SENSITIVE — FOR INTERNAL GOVERNMENT USE ONLY
>
> PROTECTED FROM DISCLOSURE UNDER FOIA EXEMPTIONS 4, 6, AND 7

Use this header if you are filing to another jurisdiction by deleting the second line, or replacing it with the appropriate phrase. Also see Part 5 on whether to go public about your submission and/or target perpetrators.

Before the submission, you can ask about how best to protect your sources. In some cases, you may be given permission not to disclose details of your sources if it would be unduly dangerous for them. In this case, you must describe in detail how they knew about the human rights violation and the targeted perpetrator(s) role in that violation as well as why they are a credible source.

For a comprehensive self-study guide in digital security, see Safeguard Defenders Practical Digital Protection guide.

3.1 Submission Checklist

All submissions, no matter which Magnitsky jurisdiction, should include the following:
Information on the perpetrators
What acts were committed that qualify them for sanctions, such as human rights violation or corruption
Evidence of the acts and of direct and/or chain-of-command responsibility for those acts
You might also include (especially for the U.S.):
An explanation why these sanctions serve the jurisdiction's national interests.

Before reading further, please check the template form for a Magnitsky sanction submission to the U.S. in section Appendix I –Template for U.S. Global Magnitsky Act Submissions.

[6] The submission should begin by identifying the perpetrator(s), either individual(s) or entity(ies). This includes all identifying information you can get such as photo, full name, date of birth, place of birth, nationality, job title, employer and ID number.

Present the evidence in narrative form in the body of the submission as well as in an annex with the evidence in full.

3.2 Deciding Who to Target

In many instances where human rights violations have occurred, there may be more than one perpetrator. There is the individual(s) who directly carried out the abuse and also superiors who were complicit in the act because they have "command responsibility".

The good news is that submissions for Magnitsky sanctions allow filings for multiple targets. The challenges for you may be in deciding whether or not to target individual(s) based on command responsibility or not and getting the information together to identify them.

It is advisable to include all identifiable perpetrators in a submission. This allows the jurisdiction to decide themselves who should be sanctioned. When targeting government officials, a good strategy is to include individuals at different levels of seniority if possible, giving the jurisdiction the flexibility to target an official at a level they think will help further strategic objectives. They might prefer to target a mid-level official first to send a message to those higher up and combine this with diplomatic pressure. If this doesn't work, they could follow up with pursuing sanctions against the higher-level official.

Command responsibility requires clear evidence of a link between the individual(s) and the violation. The more senior the official, the more difficult it will be to prove that link and the more crucial it will be to provide clear and irrefutable evidence of that link.

The first command responsibility perpetrator should be the one(s) most closely linked to the main perpetrator(s) and who have direct, day-to-day authority over the government facility where the violation(s) occurred. Also include (a) whether the individual was involved in the abuse; (b) gave orders for it be carried out; or (c) helped to facilitate it through other means.

Some jurisdictions (e.g., the U.S. and Canada) permit Magnitsky sanctions against all legal persons -- this means that enterprises and organizations -- and in the U.S., entire branches of government -- can also be targeted. For example a local Public Security Bureau/police station, or a detention center, as a whole.

A submission against a business could be based on evidence it knowingly facilitated the violation by providing material support.

A submission against an entire branch of government (e.g. Beijing Municipal Public Security Bureau) are allowed but have not yet happened. In this case sanctions would affect both the bureau and anyone associated with it. It could also prohibit sales of technology or arms to the bureau.

Two Types of Perpetrator

1.   Direct involvement. Those who directly carried out the human rights abuse

2.   Command responsibility. Those who were not physically present when the violation occurred, but who bear responsibility because they ordered and/or facilitated the act. This could include denial of medical treatment to the victim, not preventing/stopping the violation and/or declining to investigate the abuse after it occurred. Command responsibility designation requires you to identify roles and responsibilities. Cite sources and find an official organizational chart that outlines job positions in the entity. Do not only rely on "inferential claims" – that is, testimony from others that the individual "would have known" about the violation.

In deciding who to target in a submission ask yourself:

•   Should the perpetrator be sanctioned for serious human rights abuse or for corruption?

•   Is the perpetrator already being sanctioned or facing legal action for serious human rights abuse or corruption?

•   Would the interest of the Magnitsky jurisdiction be served by sanctioning the perpetrator?

3.3 ID Information

All listed perpetrators (individuals or entities) must be fully and accurately identified for a submission to be successful. The following are the types of ID information you should attempt to provide:

The minimum ID information for individuals includes their full name, date and place of birth. Other information can be extremely useful, especially an ID number (national identity card and/ or passport), but is not essential.

For command responsibility submissions, it will help your case if you provide an official chart showing the staff hierarchy. The first place to look should be the official government website. As with all evidence you collect from online sources, make screenshots of every relevant page (with the web address visible), in case the page is taken offline or moved.

Some jurisdictions (for example, the U.S.) can also sanction enterprises that are at least 50% owned by a sanctioned perpetrator. Make sure you include full information about enterprises owned by a perpetrator.

Tips on how to find this information are given in Part IV: Investigative Techniques.

8 *If the exact date is not known, you should aim to at least identify the year of birth. You could also collect statements from an associate able to reliably confirm this information; for example, a perpetrator's former classmate who could provide their age.*

Individuals	Entities
• Full name	• Enterprise name (in English as well as Chinese if two separate names exist)
• Any known aliases and former names (if relevant)	• Enterprise address
• Date of birth (at least year of birth)	• License/registration numbers/sector specific ID codes, if possible.
• Place of birth	
• Work address	
• Home address	
• Nationality	
• Job title	
• ID numbers (national ID card and passport)	
• Gender	
• Identifying photograph	
• Identifying photograph	
• Any banking information	

3.4 Building Your Case

Collecting Evidence

After you have listed all perpetrators and collected all available ID information on each of them, your next task is to build your case.

You will need to provide credible, verifiable and clear evidence that the perpetrator(s) are responsible for the human rights violation(s). The three key points are that: (1) the evidence should be credible; (2) investigators should be able to easily verify it; and (3) it shows clearly that the named actors are responsible.

Evidence can take different forms.

These can be:

- First-hand accounts such as personal statements and statements made to a victim's lawyer (these are the most useful);

- Medical reports, court documents, financial transaction receipts and statements given to lawyers by the victim or witnesses.

- Open source information such as reports (by NGOs, governments, intergovernmental organizations), news articles and independent journalism, and even social media posts.

Multiple sources are better and sources that come from well regarded institutions (such as the UN, Human Rights Watch, etc.) are more credible.

The key is to provide evidence that is credible and that is easily verifiable. You also want to provide as much evidence as you can from as many different credible sources as possible. A strong case will

not depend on a single source.

For this reason, multiple sources should be used. They could be about the same violation or they could be used to show a pattern of behavior.

If they are about the same violation they must be separate and independent sources. For example, an NGO's report on the violation and a New York Times' article citing that report are not separate and independent. They would only count as a single source – although you should include both.

Evidence Checklist

√ Is the information credible (are the sources both trustworthy and objective)?

√ Do you have two or more independent sources to support each claim you make in the submission?

√ Will the Magnitsky jurisdiction be able to easily verify your claims?

√ Does the evidence show a pattern of behavior?

√ Does the main evidence document a violation that took place within the past five years? (if not, it might be useful to establish a pattern of behavior)

√ Did you provide links to all supporting evidences that are online and to evidence submitted in the annex that is not available publicly?

√ Have you explained clearly how you collected the evidence from your sources?

√ Did you provide English translations for all your evidence?

√ Did you include information on any translator(s)?

Try to obtain at least two or more separate sources for your evidence about the same violation.

Additional tips

- Evidence for torture submissions will be stronger if it includes testimony to a lawyer that was given within days or a few weeks of the violation(s) taking place.

- If you are aware that evidence may not be objective, you should be direct and honest about this in the submission. For example, information that originated with another corrupt actor trying to use it for political gain.

- When your case involves torture in a detention facility, include any other evidence of separate instances of torture at the same facility. It will help your case. As with perpetrators, identifying information, such as official name, address, GPS location, maps, pictures etc., will be helpful if the submission concerns a detention center.

Your evidence should be presented in two sections: a narrative section that describes each piece of evidence and an annex that lists all the evidence you have gathered and are referencing to support your case.

In the narrative section, ensure you are as objective as possible. Do not make your own subjective claims.

Sourcing

Each and every claim must be supported by independent evidence and aim to stick close as possible to primary sources.

Source all claims by including links in footnotes to websites and/or the annex for documents not in the public domain.

Try to include a minimum of two separate sources supporting every claim made in the submission.

Primary sources

You can strengthen your case if you explain clearly why primary sources are able to provide evidence. In other words, why would they be in a position to know? Maybe they are the victim or they witnessed the violation or its effect (such as wounds on the victim). Take the time to explain why each piece of evidence is credible and why each source should be trusted.

Include where and when each testimony was provided (time and place of getting the information).

All first-hand sources should be as close to the victim as possible, such as the victim himself/herself, or a witness to the violation. If their accounts are not in English, also provide a translation with the original. Include both the original language and your translation. In addition, give brief background information on the translator(s), such as their name and level of professionalism.

If a source requests anonymity because they are afraid of being punished it is totally acceptable to keep them anonymous in your submission. In this case, you must explain who they are in general terms and how they came to know this information. For example, "[Person X] is a mid-level official who worked alongside the target during [some time period]".

Secondary sources

If you are using an NGO report as part of your evidence, include a description of how the NGO obtained the information and what sources they used. For example did they use first-hand victim testimony? Did they interview family members? What documents did they use?

Perpetrators

For perpetrators directly involved in the violation(s), clearly identify their role and what they did. Each accusation must be back by sourced evidence.

If you are also submitting a case against a perpetrator with command responsibility (for example, the leader of a detention facility), you will need to provide evidence on:

- Effective control. The individual(s) who committed the act(s) were clearly subordinates of the command responsibility perpetrator, either legally or factually.

- Actual or constructive knowledge. The command responsibility perpetrator knew or should have known that their subordinates were about to commit, were committing, or had committed the violation(s);

- Failure to prevent, halt, or investigate. The command responsibility perpetrator failed to take necessary and reasonable measures to prevent or halt the violation or to properly investigate and punish the perpetrators.

A key piece of evidence you should try to provide is an organizational chart. The chart should clearly describe the roles and responsibilities of the perpetrator(s) at the organization (for example local police station or detention center).

You should explain clearly why the perpetrator(s) should also be held accountable. Do not use subjective arguments, stick to the relationship between their role and the violation(s). If possible, include as much information you can get on their location at the time the violation(s) occurred.

Do not simply write they "would have had to have known that the violation was occurring". Provide evidence to prove this.

Patterns of Behavior

You can make your case stronger by arguing the violation(s) are part of a pattern of behavior. For example, if you have evidence that the perpetrator(s) also committed similar acts on a separate occasion, it would make your case more credible because it shows the perpetrator has a history of this type of behavior.

Note the violation that you are basing your case on should have occurred within the past five years and that either it is ongoing or at least at high risk of occurring again.

The submission is less likely to be successful if the violation is just a one-off occurrence. Although an argument that the abuse happens more generally throughout the system may also help.

Magnitsky Acts as Measures of Correction and Deterrence

It is important to remember that the purpose of the Magnitsky Act is not to seek justice for the victim nor to punish the perpetrators. Governments view the Act as a tool for correcting behavior and deterring such acts from happening again. For this reason, a submission is stronger when it shows that the acts are ongoing or that they are widespread within the system. Justice may therefore be sought in helping to change the system and protecting others from suffering similar fates.

Countries like the U.S. generally seek to produce a balanced list of Magnitsky sanctions that is reflective of abuses globally. This means they are not likely to target many individuals or entities from the same region or country. And they will attempt to cover a wide range of abuses and corruption. They are not looking to use this tool to impose country-specific sanctions (they employ different sanctions tools in that case, for example on Iran and Russia).

3.5 Making a "National Interest" Argument

The decision to issue sanctions is elective, meaning that even if you can make a compelling case that an individual is guilty of human rights violations and/or corruption, a government is not required to act. In reality, these Acts often serve as a tool for furthering national interests and you should expect the government to act only when it has determined that it is in its own interests to do so.

You will make your submission stronger if you argue that it will help advance the Magnitsky jurisdiction's interests. You would need to bring in its wider objectives and not simply reflect its stated principles of promoting and upholding human rights.

As a first approach, consider framing the impact of the sanctions from a positive perspective. You could talk about the amount of assets that could be frozen; the message that sanctions would send to the target country; how sanctions might improve regional security in the long run; how they could be used to the Magnitsky jurisdiction's advantage in negotiations with the target country.

Second, you should also counter any arguments against sanctions. Think about whether the sanctions would be viewed as "external meddling" by a foreign adversary looking to constrain the rise of China? Will they lead to more human rights abuses as an act of defiance by the target country? Will China respond by removing support from some other international arena? You must argue your case by describing how the sanctions could empower reformers and civil society.

There may be pushback from government officials (particularly from the diplomatic service) that might argue the sanctions would harm the relationship between the two countries. Here, you could argue that the value of addressing human rights abuses and corruption through sanctions far outweighs any potential damage to the relationship.

Third, you should describe how the sanctions would further the national interests of the Magnitsky jurisdiction. Remember, this is not just a blanket statement about how it is in the interests of the country to support human rights and democracy. Argue your case by explaining how sanctions would further, for example, U.S. foreign policy aims. You need to identify what its interests are and explain how your sanctions would help it achieve them.

Lastly, consider allying with another organization that is knowledgeable about the interests of the Magnitsky jurisdiction to help frame your argument compellingly to persuade them why sanctions would be in their national interest.

It should be noted that adding any corruption angle to the perpetrator's human rights violation will strengthen any submission, especially for the U.S.

National Interest Arguments for U.S. Submissions

Arguing it is in the national interests of the Magnitsky jurisdiction to impose sanctions is crucial when making a submission to the U.S.. This is an area that civil society often struggles with because it is not sufficient to simply say that since the U.S. supports human rights and democracy, sanctions are in its best interests.

Remember that Magnitsky Acts are not meant to be punitive they are corrective. In addition, the U.S. will be looking to apply sanctions in situations when they can use them to improve their leverage towards some political, strategic or economic end. So, think of these objectives when making national interest arguments.

For example, you may consider the following:

• How would sanctions improve the U.S. position vis-à-vis the target country?

• How would potential damage to bilateral relations from imposing sanctions be outweighed by the value to the U.S. in addressing the abuse?

• How U.S. long-term security interests are served when the rule of law, human rights and democracy thrive across the world and how sanctions serve this end.

• U.S. geopolitical and internal political dynamics.

• Perhaps the sanctions send a targeted message to the target government, political faction, military or security service unit while minimizing damage to the bilateral relationship?

• Would the sanctions isolate an individual spoiler who is preventing reforms that would lead to fewer human rights abuses and improvements to rule of law?

• Would the sanctions improve regional security by removing a dangerous element?

• Would the sanctions improve the U.S. position in a current diplomatic issue?

The Office of Foreign Assets Control (OFAC or Treasury Department) is more concerned with the size of the impact and/or whether the sanctions could change the behavior of the target or the government in general. Think about these concerns when you draft your national interest argument.

3.6 Exculpatory Information

It is also useful to consider whether there is any evidence that might undermine your case. This is called exculpatory evidence. For example, a report or social media post that places the perpetrator at a different location at the time the violation occurred. It will improve your credibility and strengthen your case if you include this information and argue why the evidence is not truly exculpatory.

Remember, if the Magnitsky jurisdiction decides to go ahead with sanctions it will need to make a case that would withstand all legal challenges. If they think they cannot do this, they will not go ahead with sanctions. The jurisdiction will carry out their own investigation of the case and they will also likely discover the exculpatory evidence so it is better for you to bring it out into the open first.

For the same reason, it is also advisable to be open about any areas of the case where information is missing or incomplete so you can assist the jurisdiction in their investigation.

Please carefully study PART V before you submit your request.

3.7 Filing the Submission

Send your completed submission to one or more of jurisdictions as outline in section 1.3 Who imposes Magnitsky sanctions? First, before submitting it, you need to decide whether to file it yourself, or work with a larger partner, such as Human Rights First. You should also contact the Congressional Executive Commission on China (CECC), and look into the possibility of them filing the submission on your behalf, or even to just provide input and help.

If you are submitting it yourself, to the U.S., we advise you to submit to both the Treasury and the State Department at the same time, and ensure that the two submissions are identical.

Shortly after submission follow up directly with the State and/or Treasury to request a face-to-face meeting to discuss your submission. For the State Department, contact both the Bureau of Democracy, Human Rights and Labor and the Bureau of International Narcotics and Law Enforcement Affairs.

It is not recommended to publish your submission or make any public remarks about your case at first. Doing so increases the risk your case will fail. Refer to Section 2.5 for more information on confidentiality. This is especially true if the perpetrator is not a public figure, for example detention center staff of individual police officers. However, there are exceptions, including of already public figures. If you work with a larger partner, or the CECC, they can help advice you what is the best way forward.

9 https://register.state.gov/contactus/contactusform
10 https://register.state.gov/contactus/contactusform

PART III

This section provides you with tips to help gather information on the perpetrators for your submission. It builds on information provided in Sections 3.3 and 3.4.

4.1 General

The first step is to build a profile of the perpetrator that uniquely and clearly identifies them. 'Identifiers' help us to confidently identify perpetrators in a Magnitsky filing or any other judicial or regulatory filing.

Collecting identifiers on an individual in China is difficult and risky because as a police state, China is intentionally unclear what is legally public or what is legally private information. In particular, information on officials is often regarded a state secret. Online research can be conducted outside China but it might not be possible to collect a complete list of identifiers online.

Profiling companies or other business entities is usually easier. Publicly accessible official and commercial databases are often enough to accurately identify an organization for judicial filing purposes.

Some 'identifiers' are:

- Their full name (and any variation) – ensure you double check all spellings are correct

- ID and/or passport number

- Name of employer

- Work and home addresses

- Telephone numbers

- Email addresses

- Social media accounts

- Bank account numbers,

- Names of family members

Cost may be a factor in how you decide to go about collecting identifiers. Competent research using free tools and public resources are a low-cost option. Sometimes you may need to pay fees to a commercial search or hire an investigation firm to collect further information to fill gaps.

4.2 Methodology

Research work will include some or all of the following:
Compile and analyze all the information you already have;
Make a research plan or action plan;
Conduct desktop research, remember to keep a log of each step;
Save all important online information immediately, either as a screenshot or a pdf. Sometimes web pages move or are deleted (and also keep the URL/web-address and mark what time you accessed it);
Make discreet phone inquiries. If necessary, make up an excuse for why you need the information, do not reveal you are planning a Magnitsky submission;
Make discreet field inquiries. If necessary, make up an excuse for why you need the information, do not reveal you are planning a Magnitsky submission;
Analyze all results and write the report.
Maps showing GPS and address of homes, photos of cars or license plate numbers, education background, ownership in any businesses, etc., are all useful information, beyond just name, employer and ID or Passport information. The more the better. Many times the information available will be limited, so the list of identifiers, and other information in this chapter, is a best case scenario, and for you much of this will often be missing.

4.3 Profiling individuals

In the beginning, you might only have one or two identifiers for the perpetrator, such as their name and their organization name. These are your leads. Gradually gather more information that will allow you to uniquely and accurately identify the perpetrator.
Conduct research in English and in Chinese. You may need to use further languages if the target is connected to a region that uses a different language (for example, Uighur in Xinjiang province).
Don't forget to check if there is a Hong Kong connection to the perpetrator (for example, company incorporation records and real estate information). In this case, remember that spellings in English in Hong Kong generally do not use pinyin Romanization, but one of a number of other Romanization methods. Use the correct spelling to conduct further searches.
Use each new identifier or piece of information on the perpetrator to conduct further research to lead you to additional identifiers. These could be alternative names and addresses, membership in social organizations, names of colleagues or friends, photographs in the media or private social media posts.
Treat everything you find as a new lead. You might come across an online ad or a post in an online forum where the perpetrator has written their phone number (for example a real estate ad or a chat forum about pets or sport). Once you have their phone number, use it as a keyword search term. You will be surprised what it might reveal.

4.4 Online Tools

Search engines (Clear web). Don't limit yourself to a single search engine. It is vital to use several in each of the languages you are using because different search engines produce different results and therefore different information. Use both Baidu and Google at the very least. If you find a website that is no longer working, visit this site to check earlier versions before it was taken offline.

Deep web searches. Normal search engines like Baidu and Google include only a small part of the information on the internet, maybe as little as 10%. See suggestions for search engines, and a brief explanation what 'deep web' is here.

Dark web searches. This small part of the internet is not accessible to normal search engines, and can only be accessed using the TOR browser, which anonymizes the user. This is the part of the internet with organized crime, weapon selling, drug smuggling, pedophilia and more. Using the TOR browser is very slow, because it need hide you, and therefore the dark web is almost only text based, with basic looking discussion forums. Download the TOR browser on your phone or computer. There are several guides out there to help you get started. This wiki entry has a list of various sites and their TOR addresses. You cannot load these pages with normal browsers, you must connect through the TOR network first. You can search the dark web using this special search engine, when in TOR mode.

Mobile phone number trackers. Search for these online and input the phone number. Most tools will tell you the type of number; the carrier; and the location of the phone. http://www.ip138.com/sj/ - This site will return where an inputted Chinese mobile phone number was registered (location). On the left-hand side of the home page there are many other categories to search. If this website does not help simply search for similar sites using the search term "手机电话查询".

ID number analysis. There are free online tools available that will use an inputted Chinese ID number and tell you date of birth, gender, and the place where the ID document was issued (which could be the same as where they live). https://qq.ip138.com/idsearch/ - This site will return the date of birth, residential address and where the ID card was issued from an inputted Chinese ID number. If this website does not help simply search for similar sites using the search term "身份证号码查询".

Chinese Supreme Court database on legal processes. All legal procedures, except those involving National Security or State Secrets should, theoretically, be listed in this database, located here: http://wenshu.court.gov.cn/. If the perpetrator is connected to a criminal case in China, there is a chance it may show up in this database.

Criminal litigation documents and judgments from across China. Although it is not comprehensive, and some information has been redacted, it is a very useful resource and the best website of its type. http://pkulaw.cn/

Social media. Social media is one of the richest resources we may have on the perpetrator. Search for them on all possible platforms, especially WeChat, and also search using the names of their close colleagues as that may lead you to your target or even further information on your target. Social media platforms are often used as vanity forums. Even some senior officials may drop their guard and post personal information such as contact numbers, email addresses, names of family members and close friends, alumni connections and photos. Dig deep into every detail.

Consider opening a ghost account created under an alias to access the perpetrator's account. A good researcher will have many such ghost accounts.

Social media photos (metadata). Download any relevant photo and then check its metadata. Many times people forget to remove such data, and can include time the photo was taken, what phone was used, but also the exact geographic location (GPS coordinates). Can be great to identify someone's location.

Professional platforms. Chinese-language sites are more common than their English-language counterparts (such as LinkedIn). Search all possible platforms in Chinese and English, as users may post different information on each site.

Recruitment platforms. Online recruitment platforms, such as www.zhaopin.com, are used by employers to post job ads and by job hunters to post their resumes. Resumes often yield phone numbers, addresses and email addresses. Use the job and education history information to search for colleagues, friends and alumni as well as any named referees. Research these too for additional information on the perpetrator. Recruitment platforms usually require prepayment to view and download resumes.

Alumni groups. Once you know which schools the perpetrator attended, search for whether they belong to any alumni associations. Research the association for further information on them. Consider posing as a prospective employer to contact alumni to dig for more information.

ID numbers. Finding the perpetrator's ID number and/or passport number is often the biggest challenge. Here are some ideas that might help you: if you have their address, check the local property register; if they made any legal filings or public record filings (such as a CCTV

senior officer filing a regulatory FARA document in the U.S.), check related documents; if they were involved in any court proceedings, check court documents; if the target has ownership or directorial interest in a company, check the company's public files; and if they have children at school, check school documents.

Corporate searches. Chinese officials and state employees often have connections with businesses. It used to be possible to look for company incorporation records and annual filings from the bureaus of the Administration of Industry and Commerce (AIC) with the help of a local law firm. The AIC is also sometime referred to as the State Administration of Industry and Commerce (SAIC) or the Industry and Commerce Bureau (ICB) has recently merged with the State Administration of Market Regulation (SAMR). In recent years, it has been harder to get information from the AIC, mainly to protect officials. However, the AIC still provides online search options for company registration information, both free and paid, on which information should be available on all firms across China. You should look through records of shareholders or directors and record basic information such as name, address, contact details, and some basic financials. You should be able to see changes in the shareholding structure over the years. However, this may no longer be possible for some companies.

- Search by company name only on this government website. http://gsxt.gdgs.gov.cn/. (this website is only available if your IP is inside mainland China, you can use a VPN to connect through a Chinese server.)

- This non-government website consolidates AIC and other corporate information records into a database that is also searchable by an individual's name. This could help you identify corporate affiliations. You will need to register and may also need to pay a subscription fee. www.qichacha.com

If you cannot find the perpetrator from this information, you can also try:

- Prospectuses. These should contain details of all shareholders (including for BVI entities) and for companies listed in China.

- Annual reports. These should disclose family relationships if more than one family member is involved in the company.

- Company reports. Most listed companies must file a report when certain shareholders cross investment thresholds and they should disclose who the ultimate beneficiary is. These can sometimes provide personal information.

- Chinabond.com.cn. This site lists prospectuses for loans, financial statements and other information on many mainland Chinese and Hong Kong companies, including unlisted ones that have been involved in bonds or loans. Sometimes this includes information on shareholders. Note that searching this site can be quite time consuming.

- Offshoreleaks.icij.org. This site lists hidden offshore entities. English only.

- Children abroad. Many Chinese officials and state employees send their children overseas to study and also to set up a base through which they can channel assets into real estate or bank accounts for example, in case they ever need to flee China in the future. Research the possibility that the perpetrator has children overseas. You might find their name on assets in Canada or the U.S.

Restrictions

In 2013, due diligence and anti-fraud consultant Peter Humphrey from the UK and his wife were arrested in Shanghai and falsely imprisoned for illegally acquiring citizens' information.

Since then, using the pretext of privacy protection, China has introduced more restrictions on collecting information on officials and it has become increasingly harder to conduct private investigation or due diligence work in the country.

The law was also amended to prohibit the gathering of private information from any source at all, which includes public online sources. This means that any research conducted in China on an individual is at risk of arrest and imprisonment, especially in sensitive cases.

Banned methods. China has made illegal certain investigatory methods once commonly used by private investigators (other countries also restrict these):

• Accessing mobile phone records (calls and texts);

• Tracking someone's location via their mobile phone signal;

• Accessing detailed profiles of individuals from incorporation files;

• Blanket real estate searches using an individual's name;

• Accessing border entry and exit records;

• Accessing client databases from service companies (e.g. airlines);

• Accessing bank records;

• Accessing criminal records

4.5 Conducting Research from Hong Kong

Hong Kong still has a relatively more liberal environment for conducting investigations and due diligence work despite the steady deterioration of its autonomy and human rights and encroachment on its judicial independence.

In Hong Kong, business licenses can be issued without providing detailed description of business activities. In Hong Kong, private investigation companies are not banned but you are required to apply for a license and comply with privacy laws. There is much more information on public record than in mainland China and so investigations here are easier and much safer.

The public records listed below can be legally accessed after paying a moderate fee, or for free. Visit in person, search the online database or hire an agent to conduct the search for you.

- Directorships. Input the name of the perpetrator to check whether they are an individual or shareholder of a Hong Kong-based company.

- Incorporation records. Kept in a company's registry, these will list the names and addresses of shareholders and directors, and either a complete or partial record of their ID or passport number, and names of company secretaries. The ID number may be a Hong Kong ID or their PRC ID. Access to this information often requires a fee.

- Annual returns. Kept in a company's registry, these will contain updates in incorporation such as changes in shareholding structure, shareholders and directors. Note: The street address of a Hong Kong incorporated company is often a corporate secretarial services company and not an operational address. Also, shareholders of Hong Kong companies are sometimes offshore companies (such as BVI or Cayman Islands) with the ultimate beneficiary shareholders concealed.

All the above you can search at Hong Kong Companies Registrar (English and Traditional Chinese). The most basic searches are free, but for more details, there are some (very) limited costs involved.

- Hong Kong-wide real estate. You can search against a name to trace property ownership transactions. Usually these only include transactions above a certain value (for example, HKD5 million).

- Real estate ownership. Search for the ownership details of a property.

- Litigation searches. Search judicial registries for litigation records.

- Criminal records. There are privacy restrictions attached to searching criminal records in Hong Kong, but local press report on most criminal trials, so try searching media.

- Marriages and deaths. Limited search is available on records of marriages and deaths.

These searches are best performed by a trained public records specialist and so you may want to hire a search company or private investigation firm based in Hong Kong to help. You may also contact Safeguard Defenders for recommendations.

Additional information that be good to have, but which there are no legal means to get, is for:

- Banking records. Attempting to retrieve banking records in Hong Kong without a court order is a criminal offence.

- Telephone call records. These are protected by privacy laws and obtaining them without a court order is a criminal offence.

PART IV

5.1 What happens after your submission?

After you file your submission, you may receive confirmation of receipt, but you should not expect to get updates on the status of the review. That includes whether or not they have decided to pursue the case by launching their own investigation. This lack of feedback can be frustrating, but it may be useful to follow up with advocacy work (described in the next section). The reason for this lack of feedback is that officials responsible for Magnitsky sanctions are essentially undertaking criminal investigations and so there is an understandable degree of secrecy. They do not want the perpetrator to know they are being investigated to prevent them from taking steps to avoid punishment (such as hiding assets).

It is possible the Magnitsky jurisdiction will contact you with a request for further clarification. This likely indicates they are looking into the case, but if you do not receive such a request it does not necessarily mean your filing has failed. Depending on the jurisdiction and type of sanctions, you may only hear that your submission had been successful once the sanctions are publicly announced. Remember, if the perpetrator(s) were not listed in the first list of designations released following your submission, it does not mean that they will not be listed later. Political factors or further research may cause delays.

There is no published list of those sanctioned with entry or visa bans by Canada and the U.S., so you will not necessarily know if you were successful in this regard. Some sanctions issued can be found on this website.

Why Magnitsky submissions are important even if unsuccessful

The very high threshold of proof required, political factors and the limited resources of jurisdictions to investigate unfortunately means that the majority of submissions will be unsuccessful. So why bother?

They are important because they are potentially effective tools for promoting systemic change. Some will be successful and it is critical that civil society make an official record of acts being committed. Every successful submission has a chance of deterring future violations.

Even when sanctions weren't imposed, the information in the submission may inform and influence a wide range of diplomatic actions that the jurisdiction may take towards China.

5.2 The role of advocacy in Magnitsky filings

Whether post-submission advocacy is helpful or not depends on the jurisdiction but it is recommended for submissions to the U.S.

In the U.S., the executive branch is not obliged to impose sanctions requested by Congress so legally it does not have to respond to advocacy from lawmakers. However, it usually does. Advocacy work can be counterproductive if it is not backed up by strong evidence and it can potentially damage the reputation of you and your organization for any future submissions.

If you feel your case is strong, advocacy is more likely to be beneficial. Advocacy work should be started shortly after submission. However, keep the submission confidential from the public unless a more experienced partner, such as the CECC or Human Rights First, advises against it. It can also be helpful to enter into conversation with other human rights NGOs to consider joint or coordinated actions, either sharing the burden of private advocacy or through joint-statements and public actions later in the process. Reach out to members of Congress/Parliament who have publicly expressed concern about human rights or issues in China. Your goal is to lobby these members to submit a written request to the government investigative body that it pays close attention to your submission.

As a general rule, do not make your submission public unless instructed to do so. Jurisdictions that suspect the target is aware of the submission will be less likely to take action. It is recommended to partner with an organization that has a presence in the Magnitsky jurisdiction to help with advocacy. It is best if they have an existing relationship with politicians. Having a physical presence in the jurisdiction means they can arrange face-to-face meetings that are more effective in advocacy work. They will also be better informed on developing local media advocacy strategy, which can help at a later stage in the process.

Make sure to consider advocacy and lobbying before filing your submission, and have a strategy for advocacy, both related to how you submit it, and what to do after, to increase the chances that your submission will be successful. The advocacy strategy should be written down and available to share with partner organizations. A good advocacy strategy should include short, medium, and long-term planning.

For submissions in the U.S., the organization Human Rights First specializes in advocacy supporting Magnitsky submissions, while the Congressional-Executive Commission on China (CECC) is a natural partner as well.

Important to consider before filing

The starting point for this section is the United States, but it will also include information on the UK and Canada, part of which, in general, also apply to other parliamentary systems that may adopt Magnitsky Acts in the future.

As stated before, there is outreach to do before you file your submission, such as the political section of the country's embassy in China, to ensure they are aware of the coming submission, and in some cases, they might want to help or work with you to make the submission. The U.S. embassy political section is likely to express interest in the process and can be a valuable early resource. There may also be special commissions (for the U.S., the Congressional-Executive Commission on China – CECC) and parliamentary groups that you can reach out to beforehand for assistance, to get feedback or help on how to best make the submission, and again, in some cases, such bodies might want to work with you to make the submission, or even make it on your behalf. If you lack existing contact or communication with Congressional groups it might instead require you to seek support from partner organizations to establish communication or legitimacy.

There are also international NGOs that can be of assistance, especially for submissions to the U.S. or Canada, and may also be able to make the submission for you. One such group is Human Rights First, which has taken the lead to provide such help. Other smaller but China specific groups also exist, such as the Network for Chinese Human Rights Defenders.

Only after considering and reaching out to such bodies, as much as you can, should you file your submission.

5.3 How to establish contact and communicate effectively with the state

Submitting to both the U.S. and Canada is straightforward: all you have to do is email the body in charge of Magnitsky sanctions. Your submission will be reviewed whether or not you receive confirmation of receipt. Again, it may help to notify or cc the embassy political officer or other influential stakeholder who can follow up on your behalf or obtain unofficial confirmation or receipt.

Depending on the country, you have several potential contact points that could assist your submission. In general, there are 5 areas that could help:

1.   The department(s) receiving the application
2.   The embassy in the target country
3.   Individual Congressional/ Parliamentary members
4.   Specific committees or groups with Congress/Parliament that deals with issues related to your submission, such as rule of law, foreign affairs, human rights, corruption, etc.
5.   International NGOs working with the Magnitsky Act

After making your submission, it is recommended that you follow up your submission with a request for confirmation of receipt if you did not receive one. If you have a physical presence in the country, you could also request a face-to-face meeting to discuss your submission. If you have no chance to be in the country in question, which is unlikely, a better strategy would be to partner with another organization – such as Human Rights First, so that they can request such meetings.

5.4 Lobbying Bodies to Approach

After the submission has been made, it's time to use lobbying and advocacy to build momentum for your submission, to increase its chances for being accepted. All the suggestions given here can also, in some cases, be used before you make the submission, as discussed in the text box above.

To identify members of the country's government that may be sympathetic to your cause, there are many ways to proceed. The easiest method is to check relevant news and identify which individuals in congress or parliament, or which bodies within congress or parliament, has been pushing for action related to your issue, region or country. Twitter is also a helpful resource to see which congressmembers or parliamentarians are speaking out publicly about these issues. A more difficult and time-consuming way is to use existing resources and lists over members of parliaments, lists of congressional bodies, etc. (See contacts and links further below).

Regardless, you need to identify those that share your cause and may be willing to assist. Google/Baidu and other search engines will be of great help to quickly identify those active on China and Human Rights issues, or those active in pushing for use of the Magnitsky Act. You may want to consider setting up a Google Alert or other alert notification for key words relevant to your campaign, such as the name of the target official.

> **Note:** In general, Committees and Commissions are official bodies of the government. Groups and Association are voluntary formations in congress or parliament by individual members who focus on an special issue or

region or country. For Groups and Associations, see the warning at the end of this section. In general, you want to reach Committees and Commissions.

For the United States

All of these resources are in English only, or have no Chinese version. However, a good browser will offer automatic translation to Chinese, which will be enough to be able to use them to your advantage anyway. To avoid repetition, NGOs and Congressional groups etc. mentioned before will not be repeated, but you will find many suggestions already in this manual.

House of Representatives: https://www.house.gov/representatives

Senate: https://www.senate.gov/senators/How_to_correspond_senators.htm

Each name of a congressperson will direct you to his personalized subpage on which you can find their contact details as well as their areas of interests.

The same research can be done for both Representatives and Senators on Congress.gov. It is the official website for U.S. federal legislative information. The Members directory (https://www.congress.gov/members) will allow you to select a member and look for specific keywords related to him.

For example, when looking at Senator Ted Cruz , and then typing "China" in the search bar at the top of the screen, you can view all resolutions and bills related to the senator, which will give you useful information on the positions of the senator on the country or his interest in the issue at stake. It will also, for example, list any co-sponsors for this legislation, which provides names for additional advocacy contacts.

You can also identify commissions and

committees within the U.S. Congress that deal with specific issues. One such commission, the CECC has been mentioned numerous times in this manual, but there are others, such as for Foreign Affairs, Intelligence, the Tom Lantos Human Rights Commission, and many more. Which ones are best suitable to you may vary depending on the violations at the core of your submission, or what types of perpetrators are involved.

For Canada and the United Kingdom

Just like with the U.S. Congress, parliamentary systems use a number of specialist bodies, both geographically and per issue. It will be key to identify suitable parliamentary groups to approach. As with the U.S., these websites will not have Chinese language, but your browser should be able to automatically translate them into Chinese.

For any other country, the most important part and resource is a simple search online for which groups or members of parliament have taken an active role about the issue your submission is about, or about China and Human Rights more generally as a starting point.

For Canada, you need to look at both Parliament and Global Affairs Canada (leading its diplomatic service). The best starting point is the Subcommittee on International Human Rights of the Standing Committee on Foreign Affairs and International Development (SDIR), which can be found here: https://www.ourcommons. ca/Committees/en/SDIR/Members.

You can use government websites to find lists of Senators, https://sencanada. ca/en/senators/#sch, as well as lists of committees, https://sencanada.ca/en/ committees/ridr/42-1. Besides committees, there are also a wide range of parliamentary

groups (associations), covering specific issues or areas, and you can find more information on that here https://www. parl.ca/diplomacy/en/associations.

In the UK, there are likewise numerous resources to help you find the most relevant people and groups within parliament. You can find a list of members of parliament here, https://www.parliament.uk/mps-lords-and-offices/mps/ and a list of "Lords" (Senators) here https://www.parliament. uk/mps-lords-and-offices/lords/.

There is a joint committee on Human Rights, https://www.parliament.uk/business/ committees/committees-a-z/joint-select/ human-rights-committee/contact-us/.

Further, in 2019, the Foreign Affairs Committee (www.parliament.uk/facom) published a critical report against China and its poor Human Rights records. On this site you can find a list of parliamentarians who wrote it, and conclude that they are likely to take a pro-human rights stance on China. Hence, those are suitable members to consider approaching.

There is also an All Party Parliamentary China Group (APPCG), but we advise you to avoid contacting any member of it before you first search about the individuals and see that they have had a critical view on Chinese Human Rights. To understand why, see the warning box below. There is a very long list of such "All-Party Parliamentary Groups" dealing with many kinds of issues, and you can find a list here https://www.parliament.uk/mps-lords-and-offices/standards-and-financial-interests/ parliamentary-commissioner-for-standards/ registers-of-interests/register-of-all-party-party-parliamentary-groups/. Some might also be of relevance to you.

Note: The UK has publicaly stated their set procedures for civil society to file submissions for Magnitsky sanctions will be established and published after the conclusion of Brexit. Check back for news on this as Brexit is concluded.

Both Labour and the Conservative Party also have their own groups that may be of relevance. The Conservative Party's human rights commission has been especially active, and often critical of China's poor respect for Human Rights, which also has a website here http://www.conservativehumanrights.com/.

As with the United States, it is valuable to connect with the local embassies in Beijing for the United Kingdom, Canada, or other countries in which you are filing Magnitsky submissions.

Warning: Any "friendship group" within parliament is likely to be very heavily pro-CCP, and are often focused solely on economic exchange. Unless you find evidence to the contrary, do not approach them and do not expect them to be helpful. In fact, they might actively try to undermine you.

Additional information

U.S.

- ENGLISH. Global Magnitsky Act (English): https://www.congress.gov/bill/114th-congress/senate-bill/284/text

- CHINESE Global Magnitsky Act (unofficial Chinese translation from China Human Rights Accountability Center): https://china-hrac.blogspot.com/p/quan-qiu.html

- ENGLISH Executive Order 13818: https://www.whitehouse.gov/presidential-actions/executive-order-blocking-property-persons-involved-serious-human-rights-abuse-corruption/

- ENGLISH State Department Page on Global Magnitsky Act: https://www.state.gov/global-magnitsky-act/

- ENGLISH Treasury Department Page on Global Magnitsky Act: https://www.treasury.gov/resource-center/sanctions/Programs/pages/glomag.aspx

- ENGLISH NGO Submission Template for U.S. filings (prepared by Human Rights First): https://www.humanrightsfirst.org/sites/default/files/GloMag-Submission-Template.pdf

- CHINESE Chinese Human Right Defenders page on U.S. Global Magnitsky Act: https://www.nchrd.org/2019/06/%E5%85%A8%E7%90%83%E9%A9%AC%E6%A0%BC/

- ENGLISH Human Rights First on Global Magnitsky Act: https://www.humanrightsfirst.org/topics/global-magnitsky

- CHINESE Human Rights Watch on Global Magnitsky Act: https://www.hrw.org/zh-hans/news/2017/09/13/309262

- CHINESE Youtube Tutorial by Dr. Han Lianchao "How to Use the Global Magnitsky sanctions mechanism to combat human rights abusers": https://www.youtube.com/watch?v=4QUSfOAHI2Q

- ENGLISH Helsinki Commission Global Magnitsky Act How-To Guide: https://www.csce.gov/sites/helsinkicommission.house.gov/files/Global%20Magnitsky%20How-To%20Designed%20Final%20Updated%20with%20Info.pdf

- ENGLISH Helsinki Commission Workshop on the Global Magnitsky Act: https://www.csce.gov/sites/helsinkicommission.house.gov/files/GetAbusersandKleptocratsSanctioned UnderMagnitsky

Canada

- ENGLISH Justice for Victims of Corrupt Foreign Officials Act: https://laws-lois.justice.gc.ca/eng/acts/J-2.3/FullText.html

- ENGLISH Special Economic Measures Act: https://lois-laws.justice.gc.ca/eng/acts/S-14.5/

- ENGLISH Global Affairs Canada Magnitsky Law: https://www.international.gc.ca/world-monde/international_relations-relations_internationales/sanctions/victims_corrupt-victimes_corrompus.aspx?lang=eng

United Kingdom

- ENGLISH Sanctions and Anti-Money Laundering Act 2018: https://www.legislation.gov.uk/ukpga/2018/13/contents

- ENGLISH Criminal Finances Act 2017: http://www.legislation.gov.uk/uksi/2018/78/made

- ENGLISH Parliament Report on Magnitsky Legislation: https://researchbriefings.parliament.uk/ResearchBriefing/Summary/CBP-8374#fullreport

Estonia

- ENGLISH Act on Amendments to the Obligation to Leave and Prohibition on Entry Act: https://www.riigiteataja.ee/en/eli/517012017004/consolide

Resources for identifying perpetrators

- LinkedIn: Linkedin.com

- Chinese Supreme Court database on legal processes in China: http://wenshu.court.gov.cn/

- Chinese recruitment platform: www.zhaopin.com

- Administration of Industry and Commerce: http://gsxt.gdgs.gov.cn/

- Business data: www.qichacha.com

- Telephone numbers: http://www.ip138.com/sj/

- ID numbers: https://qq.ip138.com/idsearch/

- Litigation records: http://www.pkulaw.cn/

- Global company data: https://opencorporates.com/ (good starting point for finding people and companies globally – also free)

- Legal & business research: LexisNexis.com (good for searches on people)

- Hidden offshore entities: https://offshoreleaks.icij.org/

- Loan prospectuses, financial statements: www.chinabond.com.cn (also other info on Chinese/HK companies)

Appendix I – Template for U.S. Global Magnitsky Act Submissions

Human Rights First have produced the templates below for submissions to the U.S. made to the U.S. departments of State and Treasury. Conversations with officials in the U.S. government have confirmed that they welcome and are familiar with this structure so we recommend you use this template or follow its structure.

The English language template is available online at: https://www.humanrightsfirst. org/sites/default/files/glomag-model-case-submission-template-18-08-06.pdf

The Chinese language template is available online at:

https://safeguarddefenders.com/zh-hans/node/206

Global Magnitsky Human Rights Accountability Act as implemented by Executive Order 13818 Submission Template

- Text in italics are guidelines and information.

- Text under ***SAMPLE TEXT**are samples, showing how such a submission can be written.

Section 1. Perpetrator Information

*Be consistent in names of entities and roles and use formal names to the extent possible.

When available, pro bono counsel should run the perpetrators through WorldCheck or a similar screening database to obtain any additional identifying information that may be available.

Where the submission alleges responsibility due to an individual's status as a leader or official of an entity that perpetrated the alleged acts (a sanctionable status under EO 13818), the NGO should seek to include an organizational chart and as much other background information as is available to illustrate the manner in which officials within various entities or departments have authority over the ultimate perpetrators of the human rights abuses or corruption.

SAMPLE TEXT

Insert photo here

Full Legal Name of Perpetrator: Colonel John Smith

Country: Generica

Title or Position: Director-General of Ministry of Security (since July 2016); former Director of the Directorate of Criminal Interrogation (2015)

Date of Birth: 12/14/1971

Other Known Personal Identifiers (passport number, address, etc): located in Metropolis, Central Province; Passport 66666666; Generica identification number 3333333

Insert photo here

Full Legal Name of Perpetrator: Colonel Edward Doe

Country: Generica

Title or Position: Director of the Directorate of Criminal Interrogation (since January 2015)

Date of Birth: 10/09/1980

Other Known Personal Identifiers (passport number, address, etc): located in Metropolis, Central Province; Passport 9999999999; Generica identification number 222222222

Section 2. National Interest Argument & Summary of Impact

Given that use of Global Magnitsky Act (GMA) sanctions authority is elective, the U.S. government must be convinced that it is in the U.S. national interest to sanction a particular individual or entity. Use this section to assess and describe the impact of a sanctions designation.

While the rationale for a particular designation should include that the U.S. government should uphold its stated commitment to promoting human rights and fighting corruption (as noted in the preface to EO 13818), the most compelling arguments will also include why a particular designation will work to advance U.S. interests and international peace and security more broadly. Such arguments could include: the ways in which sanctioning a particular individual or entity could send a targeted message to a government, government faction or military unit, isolate an individual spoiler, curb illicit finance, limit future human rights abuses within a particular unit, improve a security situation, and/or provide leverage in a diplomatic discussion. They may also include an assessment of financial assets that could be frozen/blocked when an individual is placed on OFAC's "Specially Designated Nationals"(SDN) list. As applicable, the summary of impact should also seek to explain how sanctioning the perpetrator(s) in question could deter similarly situated actors from engaging in human rights abuses and/or corruption.

SAMPLE TEXT

The Generic Security Service (GSS) is organized under the Ministry of Security (MoS) of the People's Republic of Generica, as reflected in the attached MoS Organizational Chart. Human Rights for Generica (HRG) has compiled the details of individual cases of torture by the GSS, which are attached as Annex A.

As demonstrated through these individual cases, the GSS has engaged in a pattern and regular practice of human rights abuses in Generica over an extended period of time, including routinely throughout the past five years. The pattern shows that individuals are arrested and brought to the GSS, where they are tortured for a number of hours or days, exceeding multiple months in some cases. The torture inflicted by the GSS has regularly included severe beatings, sleep deprivation, threats to family members, withholding food and water, forced standing and other stress positions, exposure to dangerously cold temperatures, sexual abuse and electric shock. HRG has confirmed that at least one of the tortured individuals died in GSS custody. Detainees are most often tortured for the purpose of coercing a confession (which many claim was false and only given to end the torture), which is used in the subsequent trial against them and results in their conviction.

Charges generally relate to domestic offenses, including "participating in protests" and "illegal assembly," as well as charges of "terrorist activity," the validity of which has been called into question by credible UN experts and human rights organizations. Some of the detainees subjected to these abuses have been as young as 15. Life imprisonment and death sentences are often imposed as a result of these confessions coerced through torture.

The individuals recommended for sanction in this submission are each either currently a high-ranking officer within the MoS or GSS, or previously held a high-ranking position there. As required for designation under Executive Order 13818, each of the individual perpetrators named in this submission is or has been a leader or official of a governmental entity that has engaged in and whose members have engaged in serious human rights abuses. Moreover, the evidence discussed in this submission confirms that there is a pattern and practice of human rights abuse by the GSS that could exist only if condoned by officials at all levels of authority. Due to the widespread and regular nature of these abuses, and the fact that these incidents of torture have been well known and documented and have occurred repeatedly for a period of many years, HRG submits that each of the individuals recommended for sanction were knowingly complicit in, and knows or should know that the government entities they have led, or their subordinates within those entities, have been engaged in ongoing human rights abuses. Furthermore, the named individuals failed to take necessary measures to halt the abuses or to investigate them in a genuine effort to impose punishment on the perpetrators. As such, HRG recommends these individuals for inclusion on the Global Magnitsky sanctions list.

It is in the U.S. government's interest to ensure that torture and other prohibited forms of ill treatment will not go unnoticed or unpunished. The GSS's abuses are well known and well documented. The designation of one or more high ranking individuals within the GSS would demonstrate the commitment and leadership of the United States to holding human rights violators accountable and ensuring that criminal convictions against individuals are aligned with international standards of fair trial rights.

These designations are aligned with the aims set out in Executive Order 13818, in which the President articulated a finding that human rights abuses outside the United States "undermine the values that form an essential foundation of stable, secure, and functioning societies" and "degrade the rule of law." While torture for any purpose is a threat to "international political and economic systems," torture for the purpose of coercing confessions is an even greater danger as it degrades confidence in the rule of law. Discarding the rule of law is a threat to global peace and security when practiced by our enemies but an even greater threat when openly tolerated by our allies. Notwithstanding Generica's cooperation with the United States on regional security initiatives, the GSS is clearly engaged in systematic and widespread human rights abuses, which are undoubtedly the type of activity the President intended to target in issuing Executive Order 13818. To overlook such blatant and well documented abuses by the GSS could call into question the sincerity of the United States' commitment to the principles of the Magnitsky sanction regime and the earnestness with which the United States is employing these sanctions. GSS designations would send a bold message that the United States does not employ the Magnitsky act as a method of impugning our adversaries but will hold even our closest allies to account when it comes to serious human rights abuses.

Furthermore, as described in multiple analyses conducted by credible analysts, Generica's domestic counterterrorism policies, including instances of torture perpetrated by members of the GSS, are having the effect of alienating, and in some cases radicalizing, members of Generica's minority population. Debriefs of Generica fighters returning from the Middle East have shown that roughly 80% of radicalized militants elected to take up arms due to a sense of personal and communal grievance driven by the Government of Generica's repressive policies. Sanctioning members of the GSS shown to have engaged in or directed torture would send a powerful signal that the U.S. government finds the Government of Generica's actions not only illegal, but also strategically counterproductive. Given Generica's key role in the fight against regional violent extremism and security partnership with the United States, the U.S. government could consider combining sanctions designations with diplomatic outreach and security sector assistance aimed at strengthening elements of Generica's security services known not to have engaged in torture.

Section 3. Case Type

Specify the type of case you are documenting. EO 13818 allows the U.S. government to sanction any foreign person determined by the Secretary of the Treasury, in consultation with the Secretary of State and the Attorney General:

1. To be responsible for or complicit in, or to have directly or indirectly engaged in, serious human rights abuse.

2. To be a current or former government official, or a person acting for or on behalf of such an official, who is responsible for or complicit in, or has directly or indirectly engaged in:

   (1) corruption, including the misappropriation of state assets, the expropriation of private assets for personal gain, corruption related to government contracts or the extraction of natural resources, or bribery; or

   (2) the transfer or the facilitation of the transfer of the proceeds of corruption.

3. To be or have been a leader or official of an entity, including any government entity, that has engaged in, or whose members have engaged in, serious human rights abuse, corruption, or the facilitation of the transfer of the proceeds of corruption relating to the leader's or official's tenure.

4. To have materially assisted, or to have attempted to have materially assisted, in human rights abuse or acts of corruption conducted by a foreign person, or to have materially assisted, or to have attempted to have materially assisted, any person previously designated under the EO.

SAMPLE TEXT

HRG submits that these perpetrators are subject to sanction under Executive Order 13818, Section 1(a)(ii)(C)(1) as current or former "leaders or officials" of "an entity…that has engaged in, or whose members have engaged in" serious human rights abuses.

Section 4. Summary of Evidence

- Provide a narrative of the facts surrounding the case you are recommending to the U.S. government, supplemented by footnoted links to supporting documents and/or annexes for documents not in the public domain.

- Include a summary description of the NGO's sources and methods of obtaining the factual information included in the submission (e.g., first-hand victim accounts, interviews with family members, documents reviewed, etc.).

- Strong cases will include as many unique sources of credible, verifiable information corroborating your claim as possible. The U.S. government prefers when evidence can be obtained and corroborated from multiple sources (in other words, a single NGO's internal information concerning a human rights violation, combined with that NGO's formal, publicly available report on the same incident(s), is likely to be viewed as a single source, and thus represent a weaker case than if the NGO's reporting can be combined with, e.g., that of a UN investigative committee).

- Where multiple perpetrators are submitted, it is helpful to detail the role(s) of each alleged perpetrator with some specificity. If the submission relies on the perpetrator's role as an official of an entity which engaged in, or whose members engaged in, human rights abuses or corruption, if possible, include the perpetrator's job description and an organizational chart in order to establish the line of authority.

- Cases submitted for crimes alleged to have occurred more than 5 years from the present are unlikely to lead to designations. As the U.S. government needs to show that the activity in question is likely ongoing (and thus that the alleged perpetrator's activity can be modified), the more recent the evidence submitted, the better.

- For human rights abuse cases, or cases in which you are recommending that a leader or official in a particular unit be designated on account of that unit's involvement in human rights abuses, your documentation should include:

- Details on the nature of the abuse(s) and victim(s), including why the actions in question qualify as "serious human rights abuse."

  - o   Though EO 13818 eliminated the GMA's requirement that a victim of abuse be expressing/defending human rights in order to qualify under the law, you should note if the alleged abuse(s) occurred because the victim(s) were involved with human rights work or otherwise expressing their fundamental freedoms.

  - o   Note that the GMA's standard of "gross violation of human rights" was understood to be limited to instances of extrajudicial killings, torture, and rape. EO 13818 lowered this bar to "serious human rights abuse," a term less well understood, but one that includes the aforementioned crimes, and may also include prolonged detention without charges and trial, disappearance, and other flagrant denial of the right to life, liberty, or the security of the person.

- The relationship between the perpetrator and the documented human rights abuse(s).

  o Note that while EO 13818 eliminated the GMA's requirement that a leader/commander be tied directly to a particular human rights abuse through "command responsibility," stronger cases will show that the higher-level alleged perpetrator directed the abuse, could not possibly have not known about it and declined to stop it, and/or declined to investigate the abuse after it occurred.

- Any evidence demonstrating that actions alleged to have been committed by the perpetrator were not unique to the specific case(s) documented, but are indicative of a wider pattern of abuse.

  o The strongest cases against a particular perpetrator will include multiple, independent accounts of the alleged crimes (such as through witness or victim testimonies), coupled with credible reporting of a more general nature on abuses known to have occurred.

- For corruption cases, or cases in which you are recommending that a leader or official in a particular entity be designated on account of that entity's involvement in corruption, your documentation should include:

- Details on the nature of the corrupt acts, including whether they included the misappropriation of state assets, the expropriation of private assets for personal gain, corruption related to government contracts or the extraction of natural resources, bribery, or the facilitation of the transfer of the proceeds of any of these acts.

  o Note that EO 13818 lowered the GMA's standard for actions covered under the law from "acts of significant corruption" to simply "corruption." The strongest cases against a particular perpetrator will include both direct and circumstantial evidence demonstrating knowledge and intent to commit a corrupt act. In addition to witness statements, documentation may include banking records or other evidence not in the public domain.

- Information demonstrating that an alleged corrupt actor is a current or former government official, or a person acting on behalf of such an official, or a person who materially assisted, sponsored, or provided support to such an official.

SAMPLE TEXT

The GSS has previously been identified in the human rights community as responsible for frequent instances of torture and ill treatment in Generica. HRG has documented individual cases in Annex A, with the most recent reported instance of torture taking place earlier this year. Many of the individuals were arrested without a warrant, with multiple individuals reporting that the arresting forces wore civilian clothing or were otherwise unidentifiable. These officers would then transport the individuals to the custody of the GSS for interrogations, during which they would subject the individuals to torture. The methods of torture most frequently employed are beatings, electric shock, sexual assault or threats of rape, forced standing, stress positions, forced nudity, and sleep deprivation.

In addition to HRG's documentation of individual cases, several other leading human rights organizations have identified the GSS as part of a pattern of human rights abuses. Human Rights International published a report in July 2016, detailing a number of human rights abuses in Generica, including torture by the GSS. HR International noted that "[m]any detainees and former detainees allege they were tortured while under interrogation by the GSS at their facility in Metropolis." HR International's report specifically corroborates some of HRG's individual cases, including those of Jane Doe (¶2 in Annex A) and John Doe (¶3 in Annex A). Additionally, Human Rights Today published a report in 2018 which documented several cases of torture by the GSS in 2016 and 2017. Both the Human Rights International and Human Rights Today reports detail similar instances of torture, including beatings, electric shock, sexual assault, and threats of rape, accompanied by demands from the interrogators to confess to criminal acts. Other instances of individual acts of torture have been reported by the Center for Human Rights, among others.

The United Nations has also addressed cases of torture by the GSS, through various communications from the Human Rights Council Special Procedures Offices on individual complaints submitted to the Special Procedures Offices ("SPOs"). As early as 2012, the SPOs were sending communications to Generica concerning reports of torture by the GSS – that year, two Special Procedures mandate holders sent an Urgent Appeal concerning the torture of John Doe by the GSS. Following his torture, Mr. Doe was charged with "unlawful assembly," a blatant violation of the right of freedom of expression. In a communication to the Generica government earlier this year, the Special Procedures office noted reports of the torture and ill treatment of Jane Doe (¶2 in Annex A). In another communication in 2017, the Special Rapporteur on torture and other cruel, inhuman or degrading treatment or punishment detailed reports of abuse and torture committed by GSS officers in the case of James Smith (¶5 in Annex A).

Finally, investigative reporting undertaken by credible press outlets, including the New York World and German news weekly Heute Zeitung has independently corroborated instances of torture by the GSS, including in facilities known to have held Jane Doe and John Doe.

Section 5. Application of Executive Order 13818

The application of EO 13818 to the particular facts included in the submission may be left to pro bono counsel to complete.

Be sure to include discussion of any references to external definitions or sources that may be used to interpret the terms in the EO and application to any particular case.

If there have been prior similar designations under the GMA, those should be discussed here as well.

The roles of the individual perpetrators recommended for designation should be discussed in as much detail as possible, along with specific references to their wrongdoing where available. If they are being recommended based on command responsibility, take care to describe with as much specificity as possible their role and the extent to which they have (or had) control over and/or involvement in the activities of those who directly participated in abuses.

SAMPLE TEXT

1. Serious Human Rights Abuses

Executive Order 13818 subjects current or former "leaders or officials" of foreign governmental entities to sanction where the entity at issue or its members have engaged in "serious human rights abuses." While the Order does not define this term, it is clear that egregious and widespread abuses such as those observed to have been committed by the GSS meet this standard. At a minimum, "serious human rights abuses" would include "gross violations of internationally recognized human rights," defined in the Foreign Assistance Act of 1961 to include "torture or cruel, inhuman, or degrading treatment or punishment, prolonged detention without charges and trial, causing the disappearance of persons by the abduction and clandestine detention of those persons, and other flagrant denial of the right to life, liberty, or the security of person."

The actions taken by individuals within the GSS (including those individuals listed as perpetrators) have shown a pattern of abuse, torture, and ill treatment that has continued from at least 2010 until the present. These actions constitute torture under the U.S. definition, as they were carried out by government officials acting under the color of law, and they were intentionally inflicted to cause severe physical or mental pain or suffering upon the individuals in their custody. However, the U.S. definition applies only to perpetrators and acts under the territorial or personal jurisdiction of the United States. As such, the international definition must also be considered, notably that found in the Convention Against Torture and Other Forms of Cruel, Inhuman or Degrading Treatment or Punishment (CAT). These actions also meet the definition of torture under the CAT, as they were intentionally inflicted by public officials for the purpose of obtaining confessions, intimidation, or punishment. As such, these cases meet the threshold of a "serious human rights abuse" and HRG hereby submits these individuals to be considered for sanctions under the Global Magnitsky Act for their membership in a government entity that has perpetrated these abuses.

2. Roles of the Individual Perpetrators

Executive Order 13818 provides for the sanction of individuals who are "leaders or officials" of governmental entities engaged in serious human rights abuses "relating to the leader's or official's tenure." As explained previously, the GSS is organized under the Ministry of Security of Generica, as reflected in the attached Ministry of Security Organizational Chart. Each of the perpetrators named in this submission held an officer level or otherwise leadership position within the Ministry of Security or the GSS specifically during the period in which the severe human rights abuses detailed above and in the accompanying evidence were perpetrated. Moreover, the evidence discussed in this submission confirms that there is a pattern and practice of human rights abuse by the GSS that could exist only if condoned by officials at all levels of authority. Due to the widespread and regular nature of these abuses, and the fact that these incidents of torture have been well known and documented and have occurred repeatedly for a period of more than several years, HRG submits that each of the individuals recommended for sanction were knowingly complicit in, and knows or should know that the government entities they have led, or their subordinates within those entities, have been engaged in ongoing human rights abuses. Furthermore, the named individuals failed to take necessary measures to halt the abuses or to investigate them in a genuine effort to impose punishment on the perpetrators.

Section 6. Discussion of Contrary Evidence/Arguments

Do not omit any known contradictory, countervailing, or exculpatory evidence. Please note any such evidence and reasons why your case still meets the law's "reason to believe based on credible information" standard.

Assume that any arguments and/or evidence that is public or available to the government of the designees' country will be shared with the U.S. agencies charged with reviewing these designations. As such, it is advantageous to address such arguments directly in these submissions as it is unlikely that we will receive another opportunity for rebuttal.

In particular, discuss why any contrary statements by the Government regarding their human rights record or efforts to address human rights complaints domestically should not be credited and provide citations to evidence, where available.

SAMPLE TEXT

HRG is not aware of any contradictory, countervailing, or exculpatory evidence concerning the alleged responsibility of Col John Smith and Col Edward Doe for acts of torture committed by GSS members under their command. While the Government of Generica has routinely denied that members of the GSS commit torture, HRG finds these claims lack credibility given the extensive documentation of such acts by credible bodies, as referenced throughout this submission.

APPENDIX

APPENDIX

Appendix II – Key information on each jurisdiction's Magnitsky Act

Canada

Legislation: The Justice for Victims of Corrupt Foreign Officials Act (Sergei Magnitsky Law) (hereafter, "SML") adopted 18 October 2017 and the Justice for Victims of Corrupt Foreign Officials Regulations (hereafter, "SML Regulations"); The Special Economic Measures Act (SEMA)

Regulatory authority: The Governor-in-Council (Cabinet) – namely Global Affairs Canada (GAC) under the direction of the Minster of Foreign Affairs

Violations actionable: gross violations of internationally recognised human rights; acts of significant corruption.

As set out in subsection 2 of the SML, activities actionable include

1. where a foreign national is responsible for or complicit in extrajudicial killings, torture or other gross violations of internationally recognized human rights committed against individuals in any foreign state who seek (i) to expose illegal activity carried out by foreign public officials, or (ii) to obtain, exercise, defend or promote internationally recognized human rights and freedoms, such as freedom of conscience, religion, thought, belief, opinion, expression, peaceful assembly and association, and the right to a fair trial and democratic elections;

2. A foreign national acts as an agent of or on behalf of a foreign state in a matter relating to an activity described in (1);

3. A foreign national, who is a foreign public official or an associate of such an official, is responsible for or complicit in ordering, controlling or otherwise directing acts of corruption – including bribery, the misappropriation of private or public assets for personal gain, the transfer of the proceeds of corruption to foreign states or any act of corruption related to expropriation, government contracts or the extraction of natural resources – which amount to acts of significant corruption when taking into consideration, among other things, their impact, the amounts involved, the foreign national's influence or position of authority or the complicity of the government of the foreign state in question in the acts; or

4. A foreign national has materially assisted, sponsored, or provided financial, material or technological support for, or goods or services in support of, an activity described in (3).

Who can be sanctioned: any foreign national

Possible sanctions: asset freezes; entry bans

Under the SML, persons in Canada and Canadian-incorporated entities and Canadian citizens outside Canada are prohibited from:

- Dealing, directly or indirectly, in any property of a designated foreign national;

- Entering into or facilitating, directly or indirectly, of any financial transaction related to a dealing in property of a designated foreign national;

- Providing financial services or any other services to, for the benefit of, or on the direction or order of, a designated foreign national;

- Acquiring financial services or any other services for the benefit of, or on the direction or order of, a designated foreign national;

- Making available any property to a designated foreign national or to a person acting on his or her behalf.

Process for designating individuals/entities: designations under the SML are published through the SML Regulations.

The Governor-in-Council (Cabinet) may, by order, authorize the Minister of Foreign Affairs to impose sanctions. These orders must be tabled in each House of Parliament within 15 days after made. As stipulated in Clause 4 of the SML, the Governor-in-Council can make orders provided s/he "is of the opinion that the foreign national is responsible for, or complicit in, extrajudicial killings, torture or other gross violations of internationally recognized human rights against whistle-blowers or human rights defenders". It is not clear what basis may be used for this "opinion".

As with the U.S., Canada imposes sanctions on a discretionary basis as a tool for influencing behaviour. This means you must make the case that sanctions would help serve Canada's national interests as well meeting evidentiary standards. Based on past behavior, sanctions are also more likely when they are part of concerted multilateral efforts with Canada's main international allies (i.e., the U.S. and the EU).

Global Affairs Canada (GAC) is responsible for the administration and enforcement of SEMA and its regulations. GAC, however, is not an investigative department and does not have direct enforcement powers. If GAC decides sanctions should be enacted, it drafts regulations and the legal opinions interpreting Canada's obligations thereunder.

Unfortunately, GAC does not offer detailed explanations for how it decides on sanctions. Following a decision to sanction, the designation process must pass through the Cabinet and the Treasury Board and can be a lengthy process.

Process for NGO filings: NGOs can submit their filing by email to: sanctions@international.gc.ca. Submissions can be made at any time and confirmation from GAC should not be expected. Following submission, you can email the office of the Minister of Foreign Affairs (check the Parliament website for current minister's address at www.ourcommons.ca/Parliamentarians/en/ministries) to request that specific perpetrators be looked at. Several NGOs could do this together, adding pressure on the government to review the submission.

Organs that receive/process filings: Global Affairs Canada.

Things to include/consider in the filing: Submissions made to GAC do not have a standard format and the government does not have a stated position on what the structure of a submission should be. The applications can be shorter than those provided to the U.S. and you do not need to put as much time into arguing the national interest argument as you would with a filing to the U.S.. Your focus here will be the quantity and quality of the evidence.

Keep your filing short and to the point. Include:

1. Perpetrator information

2. Case type & Application to the Justice for Victims of Corrupt Foreign Officials Act / Special Economic Measures Act

3. Summary of evidence

4. National interest and potential impact from sanctions

5. Evidence Annex

Evidentiary threshold: Authorities in Canada prefer open source information so include as much credible open-source information as possible. Canadian authorities tend to discount personal testimonies since they are more difficult to verify (unlike the U.S.).

Advocacy: Consider reaching out to members of Parliament and parliamentary groups, as well as groups of exiled Chinese citizens.

Estonia

Legislation: Act on Amendments to the Obligation to Leave and Prohibition on Entry Act (hereafter "OLPEA"), approved by the Riigikogu (Parliament) on 8 December 2016.

Regulatory authority: Ministry of the Interior

Violations actionable: (i) violation of human rights resulting in death or serious injury to a person; (ii) causing an individual to be wrongly convicted due to political motives.

Under Section 29.6.1 of the OLPEA, one of the bases for prohibiting entry to a foreigner includes the condition that "there is information or a good reason to believe that the [foreigner] has participated or contributed to violation of human rights in a foreign state, which has resulted in the death or serious injury of a person, the unfounded conviction of a person in an offence inspired by political motives or other serious consequences"

The criteria under which "good reason to believe" can be invoked is not clear.

Who can be sanctioned: any foreign national.

Possible sanctions: Entry ban.

Process for designating individuals/entities: The process is not entirely clear. In principle, each case would be evaluated separately by the Estonian Ministry of the Interior and appears to begin upon receipt of an application of a prohibition on entry. Who submits these applications in practice and how they may be submitted is also not clear. However, as stated in Section 31.1.1 of the OLPEA, "a governmental authority or a state agency administered by a governmental authority may make a proposal to the minister responsible [i.e. Minister of the Interior] for the area to order application of prohibition on entry". This proposal "shall contain the basis and reason for application of prohibition on entry and the circumstances set forth in subsection 31 (3) this Act. Where possible, documents in proof of the circumstances shall be appended to the proposal".

In practice, it would appear that such proposals would be likely to be put forth by the Ministry of Foreign Affairs, the Police and the Border Guard Board or the Estonian Internal Security Service. The criteria under which they make these applications and the process by which they make this determination are not clear.

Process for NGO filings: It is not whether Estonian officials accept submissions from civil society.

Organs that receive/process filings: Not clear. Ultimate filings are received by the Ministry of the Interior, but can only be submitted by other ministries.

Things to include/consider in the filing: Not clear.

Evidentiary threshold: Not clear.

Gibraltar

Legislation: The Proceeds of Crime (Amendment) Act 2018 (hereafter PCA), effective 2 February 2018.

Regulatory authority: The Gibraltar Financial Intelligence Unit (GFIU), an operationally independent and autonomous unit which consists of: (a) a "Head", represented by a senior police officer, senior customs officer or any such suitably qualified person as appointed by the Attorney General; and (b) any other officers made available to it.

Violations actionable: conduct occurring in a country or territory outside Gibraltar that constitutes or is connected with a "gross human rights abuse or violation."

Under Section 70A of the PCA, "conduct constitutes the commission of a gross human rights abuse or violation if all three of the following conditions are met:

1.   The first condition is that:

    a.   The conduct constitutes the torture of a person who has sought –

        i.   To expose illegal activity carried out by a public official or a person acting in an official capacity; or

        ii.   To obtain, exercise, defend or promote human rights and fundamental freedoms; or

* conduct that involves the intentional infliction of severe pain or suffering on another person is conduct that constitutes torture for the purposes of this subsection. It is immaterial whether the pain or suffering is physical or mental and whether it is caused by an act or omission.

    b.   The conduct otherwise involves the cruel, inhuman

or degrading treatment or punishment of such a person

2.   The second condition is that the conduct is carried out in consequence of that person having sought to do anything falling within subsection (a)(i) or (ii) above.

3.   The third condition is that the conduct is carried out –

        a.   By a public official, or a person acting in an official capacity, in the performance or purported performance of his official duties; or

        b.   By a person not falling within paragraph (a) at the instigation or with the consent or acquiescence – (i) Of a public official; or (ii) Of a person acting in an official capacity – who is instigating the conduct, or in consenting to or acquiescing in it, is acting in the performance or purported performance of his official duties.

Who can be sanctioned: public officials, persons acting in an official capacity

Conduct is connected with the commission of a gross human rights abuse or violation if it is conducted by a person that involves:

1. Acting as an agent for another in connection with activities relating to conduct constituting the commission of a gross human rights abuse or violation;

2. Directing, or sponsoring, such activities;

3. Profiting from such activities; or

4. Materially assisting such activities

* the cases in which a person materially assists activities include, but are not limited to, those where the person – (a) provides goods or services in support of carrying out the activities; or (b) provides any financial or technological support in connection with their carrying out.

Possible sanctions: asset freezes, civil recovery

According to the PCA, any property obtained through unlawful conduct will be subject to the existing civil recovery powers within the Act including the freezing of assets obtained and their subsequent forfeiture.

Process for designating individuals/entities: Unclear.

Under Article 70B of the Act, proceedings can be brought under the pretext of human rights violations when (whichever is earliest):

1. A claim form is issued;

2. An application is made for property freezing order under Section 74; or

3. An application is made for an interim receiving order under Section 81

* An interim receiving order is an order for (i) the detention, custody or preservation of property, and (ii) the appointment of an interim receiver.

Who is responsible for filing these applications and forms is not clear.

Process for NGO filings: It is not clear that NGOs can make individual requests. Any NGO requests would have to be made to the GFIU.

Organs that receive/process filings: Unclear

Things to include/consider in the filing: Unclear

Evidentiary threshold: Unclear

Latvia

The current state of legislation is unclear, suggest to avoid relying on Latvia for Magnitsky submissions at this point.

Legislation: Proposal to introduce sanctions against the officials connected to the Sergei Magnitsky case.

Regulatory authority: Ministry of Foreign Affairs

Violations actionable: Not clear.

Who can be sanctioned: It is not clear that this is an Act that can be applied to a broad set of violators of human rights. Rather, it may be specific to those involved in the Sergei Magnitsky case

Possible sanctions: inadmissibility

Process for designating individuals/entities: Not clear that there is a process

Process for NGO filings: Not clear that such a process exists

Organs that receive/process filings: Not clear

Things to include/consider in the filing: Not clear

Evidentiary threshold: Not clear

Lithuania

Legislation: Amendment to the Law on the Legal Status of Aliens

Regulatory authority: Ministry of the Interior/Foreign Ministry

Violations actionable: Violations of human rights and freedoms in a foreign country, corruption offences, money laundering, or for those on the national list of foreigners denied entry to an EU, EFTA and NATO member state.

Who can be sanctioned: any foreign national

Possible sanctions: entry ban

Process for designating individuals/entities: The Interior Minister makes a decision at the Foreign Minister's proposal. How the Foreign Minister makes this designation and the criteria that inform the decision is not clear.

Process for NGO filings: It is not clear how designations are made and what role – if any – NGOs may play in this process.

Organs that receive/process filings: Not clear

Things to include/consider in the filing: Not clear

Evidentiary threshold: Not clear

United Kingdom

Legislation: (i) The Criminal Finances Act 2017 (hereafter, CFA), which amended the Proceeds of Crime Act 2002 (hereafter, POCA) (thereby expanding the definition of "unlawful conduct" to include gross human rights abuse or violations, allowing asset freezes on human rights violators), passed 21 February 2017 by the House of Commons, receiving Royal Assent on 27 April 2017; and (ii) the Sanctions and Anti-Money Laundering Act 2018 (hereafter SAMLA), which includes gross human rights violations as a reason for imposing sanctions on a person or entity, passed 1 May 2018 by the House of Commons.

Regulatory authority: Foreign Office; Treasury, including the Office of Financial Sanctions Implementation (OFSI); Home Office

Violations actionable: gross human rights abuses or violations

"Gross human rights abuse or violation" means conduct which constitutes the torture, or cruel, inhuman or degrading treatment or punishment, of a person on the grounds that that person has sought to obtain, exercise, defend or promote human rights, or has sought to expose illegal activity by a public official. The conduct must be carried out in consequence of the person having sought to do these actions and must have been carried out by a public official or person acting in an official capacity.

Who can be sanctioned: The gross human rights abuse or violation must be carried out by a public official or a person acting in a public capacity in performance or purported performance of their official duties. Alternatively, it may be committed by another person acting with the consent or acquiescence of a public official or a person acting in an official capacity, where such consent or acquiescence occurred in the performance or purported performance of official duties.

Possible sanctions: asset freezes, civil recovery, entry bans

Process for designating individuals/entities: Sanctions seem to be imposed either by Treasury or the Foreign Office though the process for this is unclear at present. Given the newness of the SAMLA in particular, there is not much information on how gross human rights acts and violations are sanctioned. With respect to the CFA, authority rests with the Home Office, but it is also unclear which enforcement agency takes the lead in investigating and prosecuting acts related to human rights violations. Indeed, no sanctions under this legislation have been issued yet and it appears that the UK has every intention of not making use of this until its exit from the European Union is complete.

Under SAMLA, an "appropriate Minister" (i.e. Foreign Office or the Treasury) will be able to designate and sanction persons if s/he has "reasonable grounds to suspect that that person" is involved or associated with activities and considers that it is "appropriate" to sanction them. The scope of what constitutes "reasonable grounds" is unclear.

Process for NGO filings: It is not clear if NGOs are permitted to provide information and the process by which this should be carried out. It is unclear who they would contact.

Organs that receive/process filings: Not clear.

Things to include/consider in the filing: Not clear.

Evidentiary threshold: Not clear

United States

Legislation: (i) The "Global Magnitsky Human Rights Accountability Act" [hereafter Global Magnitsky Act (GMA)], 23 December 2016, Sections 1261-1265, Subtitle F, Public Law 114-328 of the FY17 National Defense Authorization Act. (ii) Executive Order 13818: "Blocking the Property of Persons Involved in Serious Human Rights Abuse or Corruption", issued 20 December 2017.

Regulatory authority: Under the Section 3 (h) of the GMA, regulatory authority for issuing regulations, licenses and orders for carrying out and authorising sanctions is vested in the President of the United States. Authority over identifying sanctionable foreign persons is assigned to the Assistant Secretary of State for Democracy, Human Rights, and Labour, in consultation with the Assistant Secretary of State for Consular Affairs and other bureaus of the Department of State, as appropriate, under Sect. 3 (i). In such instances, these persons are to be submitted to the Secretary of State for review and consideration. Under EO 13818, the President subsequently delegates authority to the Secretary of Treasury, Secretary of State and Attorney General. Treasury and State maintain separate sanction processes, but meet regularly to coordinate.

In practice, the key actors involved in carrying out sanctions are the Office of Foreign Assets Control (OFAC) under the Department of Treasury, working in coordination with the Department of State's (DOS) Office of Economic Sanctions Policy and Implementation under the Bureau of Economic and Business Affairs (responsible for coordinating DOS policy and giving guidance to the OFAC on foreign policy considerations for sanctions implementation) and the Bureau of Democracy, Human Rights, and Labour (DRL) tasked with monitoring human rights for DOS.

Violations actionable: "serious human rights abuses" and "corruption"

Under E.O. 13818, the scope of the GMA has been broadened to include "serious human rights abuse" and "corruption". This stands in contrast to the GMA, which allowed actions against individuals who: (a) have engaged in extrajudicial killings, torture, or other gross violations of human rights against individuals who either seek "to expose illegal activity carried out by government officials" or "to obtain, exercise, defend, or promote internationally recognized human rights and freedoms, such as the freedoms of religious, expression, association, and assembly, and the rights to a fair trial and democratic elections; or (b) government officials or senior associates of such officials who are engaged in, or responsible for, acts of significant corruption. Individuals who have acted as agents of, or on behalf of human rights abusers, or who have materially assisted corrupt officials, can also be sanctioned."

Thus, E.O. 13818 broadens the set of actions under which filings can be made by replacing "other gross violations" with the less narrowly defined "serious human rights abuse". However, what is not clear is what exactly would qualify as a "serious human rights abuse" as there is no written definition of this term. At a minimum, it should be understood as pertaining to acts of extrajudicial killing, torture, rape or enforced disappearance, with potential action possibly taken against cases of politically motivated imprisonment. The scope of additional acts under which the GMA may be invoked remains to be seen.

Who can be sanctioned: Sanctions can be made against any foreign person determined by relevant authorities:

1.   to be responsible for or complicit in, or to have directly or indirectly engaged in, serious human rights abuse.

2.   To be a current or former government official, or a person acting for or on behalf of such an official, who is responsible for or complicit in, or has directly or indirectly engaged in:

        a.   Corruption, including the misappropriation of state assets, the expropriation of private assets for personal gain, corruption related to government contracts or the extraction of natural resources, or bribery; or

        b.   The transfer or the facilitation of the transfer of the proceeds of corruption

3.   To be or have been a leader or official of:

    a. An entity, including any government entity, that has engaged in, or whose members have engaged in, serious human rights abuse, corruption, or the facilitation of the transfer of the proceeds of corruption relating to the leader's or official's tenure; or

    b. An entity whose property and interests in property are blocked pursuant to this order as a result of activities related to the leader's or official's tenure;

4.   To have attempted to engage in any of the activities described in the sections (1) or (2)

EO 13818 also allows sanction of any person (foreign or domestic) determined:

1.   To have materially assisted, sponsored, or provided financial, material, or technological support for, or goods or services to or in support of any activity described in sections (1) or (2) that is conducted by a foreign person;

    a. Any person whose property and interests are blocked pursuant to this order; or

    b. Any entity including any government entity, that has engaged in, or whose members have engaged in, any of the activities described in sections (1) or (2) where the activity is conducted by a foreign person;

2.   To be owned or controlled by, or to have acted or purported to

act for or on behalf of, directly or indirectly, any person whose property and interests in property are blocked pursuant to this order; or

3.   To have attempted to engage in any of the activities described in section (1) or (2)

Thus, any entity where the sanctioned person maintains an ownership share equal to or exceeding 50 percent is also subject to sanctions.

In short, the above clarifies that any non-U.S. perpetrator of a serious human rights abuse or significant act of corruption can be sanctioned as well as any person who maintained clear command responsibilities over the perpetrator(s). It further allows for sanctions against entities or individuals providing support to the aforementioned perpetrators and for the entities that may be controlled by the perpetrator(s).

Possible sanctions: blocking or revocation of U.S. visas and blocking/seizure/freezing of all U.S.-based property and interests in property of foreign persons (individuals and entities).

Process for designating individuals/entities:

⇨ **Step 1: U.S. interagency identifies potential targets**

Information on persons to be sanctioned can be made by:

- Congress

- President (Secretary of the Treasury, SOT) considers information provided jointly by the chairperson and ranking member of each of the appropriate congressional committees (House Foreign Affairs; House Financial Services; Senate Foreign Relations; and Senate Banking, Housing, and Urban Affairs)

  * Note: the names submitted by Congress do not require executive action, but as a matter of protocol generally will, to be reviewed

- Assistant Secretaries of State

- Assistant Secretary of State for Democracy, Human Rights, and Labor, in consultation with the Assistant Secretary of State for Consular Affairs and other bureaus of the Department of State may submit to the Secretary of State for review and consideration

- Foreign governments

- President (SOT) shall consider credible information obtained by other countries

- NGOs

- President (SOT) shall consider "credible information obtained by other countries and nongovernmental organizations that monitor violations of human rights"

Ultimately, the list of targets will be compiled by the State Department and the Treasury Department's Office of Foreign Assets Control (OFAC), which will be assisted by the above and other relevant U.S. interagency efforts (e.g., all regional bureaus, embassies, and relevant bureaus). NGOs may help initiate an investigation through submission of information or it may assist in ongoing investigations, but it is not essential that the NGO act for a person to end up on the designation list. While the GMA included a requirement that the Executive respond to all Congressionally submitted names, the Executive has since clarified that it is not formally required to do so through its ability to exert Executive privilege in any such investigations. In practice, however, Treasury and State will respond to any submissions formally put forth by Congress.

⇨ **Step 2: State, in conjunction with the OFAC and other U.S. interagency partners, compiles draft lists of sanction designees**

⇨ **Step 3: State sends names of potential designees to OFAC to be disseminated through the U.S. interagency**

At this point, OFAC will consult throughout the U.S. interagency on possible operational conflicts. It will also develop target packages using multiple sources of corroborated information, including drafting an evidentiary memorandum with exhibits that provide reason to believe that the target meets one or more of the designation criterion set forth in the GMA or EO 13818.

⇨ **Step 4: OFAC sends target packages to Secretary of State's concurrence, and to the Department of Justice for a litigation risk review.**

⇨ **Step 5: List of new designations is finalized.**

Treasury then prepares press documents and circulates them throughout the U.S. interagency for review. OFAC, in turn, begins technical preparations to update the Specially Designated Nationals (SDN) list and to notify consumers, especially financial institutions, worldwide.

⇨ **Step 6: OFAC Director signs Blocking Memo; OFAC issues announcement; Treasury issues press release; OFAC transmits designation to the Federal Register for publication.**

⇨ **Step 7: State writes annual report to Congress on Global Magnitsky Act implementation (10 Dec of each year).**

There is no specific timeframe for how long this process takes, though the average time to move from fact-finding to designation is around six to nine months.

Process for NGO filings: the process for submitting a petition by an NGO is straightforward.

In its simplest form, the NGO submits all relevant information to the OFAC and State Department through the designated email addresses:

- Treasury: glomag@treasury.gov

- State: globalmagnitsky@state.gov

Additionally, an NGO can lobby Congressional members directly or indirectly in the hope that they will make a request to OFAC and the State Department. This might help improve chances of the submission being successful, but it is not necessary.

There is no statutory requirement to respond to information presented by NGOs.

Organs that receive/process filings: Under E.O. 13818, final determination of whether to sanction a foreign person is made by the Secretary of the Treasury. This decision is made in consultation with the Secretary of State and the Attorney General.

In practice, the Treasury Department's Office of Foreign Assets Control (OFAC) is the subdivision responsible for evaluating and imposing financial sanctions. OFAC will determine whether there is credible evidence to justify sanctions on a foreign entity under the GMA. The Secretary of State is authorized by EO 13818 to deny sanctioned persons entry into the U.S.. The OFAC is the central office within the U.S. Department of the Treasury responsible for designating individuals and entities for sanctions. They construct the evidentiary memorandum that can, ultimately, lead to an individual being added to the Specially Designated Nationals (SDN) list.

Things to include/consider in the filing:

In general, a petition will consist of three elements (to be discussed in greater detail below).

1.   Identification of the individual(s) or entity(ies)

2.   Derogatory information

3.   Exculpatory information

However, given that the decision to issue sanctions is elective, a strong petition will also include

4.   Details on how sanctions serve U.S. interests

All information provided should be credible. State and Treasury are flexible with regard to sources that can be used. Information that can be included in the evidentiary memorandum can consist, inter alia, of: open source, NGO reports, news articles, independent journalism, court documents, medical reports, financial transaction receipts, personal testimonies. **It is important that the government is able to verify the credibility of every piece of information.** To this end, the evidence submitted will be substantially strengthened by the extent to which it can be corroborated by separate sources. Ideally, corroborating sources all know about the same kind of activity but gain the information in different ways. It is not necessary to show that the activity is ongoing, but this would strengthen your case. The violations should have occurred recently – at least within the past five years – preferably over the past year. Older information can be used to demonstrate a pattern of behaviour.

In general, the filing will undertake the following steps.

⇨ **Step 1: Identify the Target**

As a preliminary step, it is important to determine that the individual(s) and/ or entity(-ies) meet the basis for sanctions as set out in E.O. 13818.

When compiling the evidentiary file, it is important to include as much identifying information as possible. For **individuals** this should include:

- Full name

- Date of birth

- Place of birth

- Passport number(s)

- ID number(s)

- Nationality

- Gender

- Photograph

  Note: Without identifying information, sanctions cannot be imposed.

For **entities**, identifying information includes:

- Addresses

- registration license numbers

- other relevant documentation.

⇨ **Step 2: Collect derogatory information**

Derogatory information should be provided that includes the specific violations alleged. These should contain as much information as possible and should describe:

- the individual's role in the serious human rights abuse

- whether the individual had personal engagement with the abuse, gave orders that it be carried out, or helped to facilitate its occurrence through other means

Evidence could include any of the aforementioned sources. In countries without developed bureaucracies, personal accounts may be more relevant. For personal accounts, it is not necessary to provide the name of the source to the government. Rather, the government needs to know how this person obtained their information, why this person is credible, and why any documents they may provide are credible. They will want to be legally sure each piece of evidence is genuine. If there is not much official documentation, you could provide personal testimonies from victims gathered through structured interviews. Medical reports are also be helpful. The goal is to provide corroborated evidence that points to specific abusers and people with command responsibility over the direct perpetrators. Combine first-hand accounts with a solid understanding of the chain of command, so that the government can go after the person who ordered the crimes. Other good corroborative sources include the work of UN special rapporteurs or other objective, credible authorities.

In submitting evidence, the following is advised:

- Provide a narrative of the facts surrounding the case, supplemented by footnoted links to supporting documents and/or annexes for documents not in the public domain.

- Include a summary description of sources and methods of obtaining the factual information included in the submission (e.g., first-hand victim accounts, interviews with family members, documents reviewed, etc.)

- Include as many unique sources of credible, verifiable information corroborating your claim as possible.

- Be specific about roles if your submission has multiple perpetrators. If the perpetrator is an official at an entity which engaged in, or whose members engaged in, human rights abuses or corruption, include their job description and an organizational chart in order to establish they had command responsibility.

- The more recent the evidence the better

- For human rights abuse cases, or cases in which you are recommending that a leader or official in a particular unit be designated on account of that unit's involvement in human rights abuses, your documentation should include:

   o   Details on the nature of the abuse(s) and victim(s), including why the actions in question qualify as "serious human rights abuse".

      □   Make it clear if the alleged abuse(s) occurred because the victim(s) were involved with human rights work or otherwise expressing their fundamental freedoms

   o   The relationship between the perpetrator and the documented human rights abuse(s)

      □   Stronger cases will show that the higher-level alleged perpetrator directed the abuse, could not possibly have not known about it and declined to stop it, and/or declined to investigate the abuse after it occurred.

   o   Any evidence demonstrating that actions alleged to have been committed by the perpetrator were not unique to the specific case(s) documented, but are indicative of a wider pattern of abuse

      □   The strongest cases against a particular perpetrator will include multiple, independent accounts of the alleged crimes (such as through witness or victim testimonies), coupled with credible reporting of a more general nature on abuses known to have occurred.

- While command responsibility is not required, it is still advised to demonstrate command responsibility whenever possible. In general, command responsibility requires proving:

   o   Effective control: individuals who committed the violations were subordinates of the perpetrator with command responsibility, either as a matter of fact or law;

   o   Actual or constructive knowledge: they knew or should have known that subordinates were about to commit, were committing, or had committed relevant acts, given the circumstances at the time;

   o   Failure to prevent, halt, or investigate: they failed to take necessary and reasonable measures to prevent or halt the acts or to investigate the acts in a genuine effort to punish the perpetrators.

On disclosure. State and Treasury will protect sensitive sources during administrative and legal proceedings if it is clear that harm to the individual may arise if their identity is disclosed. Make it clear in your submission if this is the case. Consider contacting State and Treasury to deal with source protection concerns prior to submission.

⇨ **Step 3: Provide any exculpatory information**

It is important to include discrepancies in the case otherwise the government may doubt the credibility of your evidence. You will help your case by being totally transparent. All exculpatory information should be acknowledged and explained why it does not weaken your case. This is especially important if the evidence includes personal accounts, since the credibility of the individuals providing information will be key.

⇨ **Step 4: How sanctions serve U.S. interests**

A successful submission always makes a persuasive case that targeting the perpetrator would serve the national interests of the U.S. as well as advancing critical human rights, democracy and transparency interest. It is important to understand U.S. foreign policy toward a given country in order to build a compelling case. Helpful elements to address/consider may include:

• Counter arguments that the bilateral relationship of the U.S. and the target country is more important to U.S. interests than sanctions and potentially angering their government.

• How potential damage to bilateral relations is outweighed by the value of addressing the human rights abuses through sanctions

• How the long-term security interests of the U.S. are served when the rule of law, human rights and democracy thrive across the world and how sanctioning this particular individual serves these ends.

• Geopolitical dynamics and internal political dynamics within the country.

• Would the sanctions send a targeted message to a government, a faction of government or a specific military or security service unit while minimising damage to the bilateral relationship?

• Would the sanctions isolate an individual spoiler who is preventing reforms that would lead to fewer human rights abuses and greater rule of law?

• Would the sanctions improve a regional security situation by disabling a dangerous element?

• Would the sanctions provide added leverage in an ongoing diplomatic discussion?

Potentially as much care may be needed in thinking about how to make the U.S. interest argument as with the evidentiary case. The U.S. regards these sanctions as a tool to change behaviour and not to punish violators. Even if 50 separate cases were submitted outlining human rights abuse in China and all were strong, only a handful may end up in sanctions. This is of immense potential benefit to the bigger picture of safeguarding and promoting human rights, but it does mean that this is not an effective approach to seek justice for a specific violation.

⇨ **Step 5: Submission**

Once you have enough credible information, the file is ready for submission. Email submissions do not necessarily receive a receipt of confirmation. The Treasury and State Departments may or may not follow up for additional information. A personal meeting with U.S. government personnel can be requested by email.

There are limited resources within State and Treasury and much of this work is very labour intensive. A submission should seek to make their jobs easier. One approach may be in having NGOs working together rather than inundating it with uncoordinated submissions. Providing as much information as possible will help speed up the process (particularly with respect to corroboration). Yet, it should be as concise as possible.

* Note that just because a perpetrator has not been listed in a specific tranche, does not mean that they won't ultimately be sanctioned.

Evidentiary threshold: There is no explicitly specified burden of proof and/or evidentiary standard within the GMA. In practice, however, the evidentiary threshold is akin to requiring a "reason to believe" "based on credible information". Evidence provided should seek to exceed this threshold.

To establish a "reasonable basis" of belief that an entity has engaged in the behaviours described by the E.O., each piece of evidence must be corroborated by multiple, preferably independent sources. Credibility of the individual and/or organisation making the claim are given weight in determining credibility of information.

Cases of torture in a detention facility are strengthened when evidence can be provided that proves other activists were also tortured in the facility. In cases of command responsibility and status-based responsibility, the evidentiary threshold has been established by referencing an administrator's official job description as a means to demonstrate that s/he was supposed to know that violations were occurring and did nothing to stop such behavior.

GMA is elective, meaning that even if an evidentiary threshold is exceeded, the U.S. is not obliged to act. That is why it is important to also argue sanctions are in the country's national interests (see above).

Importantly, the government will also consider a number of issues beyond simply the strength of the case. In addition to foreign policy priorities, they may seek to go against less publicized individuals in order to ensure that the financial impact is larger. They may also consider the following strategic dimensions:

• 	Impact v. messaging. Is it punitive or preventative?

• 	One-off v. network. Should the sanction be used to bring down a specific bad actor as a punitive measure or is it designed to disrupt a larger network of behavior?

• 	Unilateral v. multilateral.

• 	Interagency approaches. Do they want to complement work undertaken elsewhere or go after targets that other agencies can't reach?

The consensus is that the U.S. is looking to deter future violations so it would help your case if you can show a pattern of abuse.